THE
BIG BOOK OF
WHOLE SCHOOL
WELLBEING

PRAISE FOR THE BOOK

Now, more than ever, it is clear that all schools need congruent and holistic approaches to supporting the mental health and wellbeing of those in their communities. This book is a rich and comprehensive compendium, with contributions from a diverse range of voices across the sector. A must-read for all educators.

Viv Grant – Director Integrity Coaching

This is exactly the book all educationalists need to read. Bringing together an amazing group of wellbeing experts, *The Big Book of Whole School Wellbeing* provides invaluable guidance at the time we need it most. As education looks to the future, here is a tool we can all use to lead well, educate well, learn well, engage well and include well.

Phillip Hedger – CEO, LEO Academy Trust

This really is a big book. The structure of leading, educating, learning, engaging and including well is a simple yet reflective take on wellbeing. You can make a difference for your stakeholders' wellbeing by kicking tokenistic approaches into touch so wellbeing becomes a genuine focus seen and felt in day-to-day actions. Hope your CPD library has a big space!

Vivienne Porritt – Leadership Consultant, Strategic Leader of WomenEd and Vice President of Chartered College of Teaching | @ViviennePorritt

It is chock-full of practical ideas, pertinent research and first-hand insights.

Dr Emma Kell – Teacher, writer, coach

Wellbeing can often be mis-interpreted, especially when considered within an educational setting, and this book rights that wrong.

Toria Bono – Primary Teacher, Evidence Lead Educator, Founder of Tiny Voice Talks

A resource that I wish had been available as I embarked on my own leadership journey.

James Hilton – Speaker and author

The big book of whole school wellbeing does exactly what it says on the tin.

Andy Mellor – National Wellbeing Director, Schools Advisory Service

EDITED BY
KIMBERLEY EVANS, THÉRÈSE HOYLE
FREDERIKA ROBERTS AND BUKKY YUSUF

THE

BIG BOOK OF
WHOLE SCHOOL
WELLBEING

SAGE Publications Ltd
1 Oliver's Yard
55 City Road
London EC1Y 1SP

CORWIN
A SAGE company
2455 Teller Road
Thousand Oaks, California 91320
(0800)233-9936
www.corwin.com

SAGE Publications India Pvt Ltd
B 1/I 1 Mohan Cooperative Industrial Area
Mathura Road
New Delhi 110 044

SAGE Publications Asia-Pacific Pte Ltd
3 Church Street
#10-04 Samsung Hub
Singapore 049483

Editor: James Clark
Senior assistant editor: Diana Alves
Production editor: Katherine Haw
Copyeditor: Bryan Campbell
Indexer: Charmian Parkin
Marketing manager: Dilhara Attygalle
Cover design: Wendy Scott
Typeset by: KnowledgeWorks Global Ltd.
Printed in the UK

Library of Congress Control Number: 2021936742

British Library Cataloguing in Publication data

A catalogue record for this book is available from the British Library

ISBN 978-1-5297-6426-0
ISBN 978-1-5297-6425-3 (pbk)

At SAGE we take sustainability seriously. Most of our products are printed in the UK using responsibly sourced papers and boards. When we print overseas we ensure sustainable papers are used as measured by the PREPS grading system. We undertake an annual audit to monitor our sustainability.

CONTENTS

ABOUT THE EDITORS

Kimberley Evans is an experienced teacher, higher level teaching assistant and heritage educator. After seeing so many people leave education due to unhappiness and workloads, she set up 'Nourish the Workplace' to make a difference to the profession she loves.

Nourish the Workplace gives schools the tools they need to prioritise and celebrate staff wellbeing. It gives every member of staff a voice and helps the school recognise their staff and their particular needs. Kimberley has worked with every type of school – primary, secondary, private, PRU and international – giving her a unique view of staff wellbeing from the ground up.

She provides CPD training to schools, individual coaching, and workshops at conferences on how to take responsibility for your own health, wellbeing and productivity. Kimberley is on the steering group for #teacher5aday, an organisation which supports and encourages teachers to take an active responsibility for their own wellbeing. She has run well-attended workshops on staff wellbeing for Optimus Education, TeachWellFest, PedagooHampshire, SouthernRocks, Cobham Hall and Resilient Rutland.

She tweets at @nourishworkplce and can also be found on LinkedIn and at www.nourishtheworkplace.com

Thérèse Hoyle has a passion for creating positive and harmonious school cultures.

For 20 years (and counting) she has worked as an education consultant, leadership coach and trainer with over 500 schools and organisations nationally and internationally.

She advises schools and school staff on positive behaviour management; creating positive playtimes; social, emotional and mental health needs of children; staff wellbeing; coaching and leadership and is an adviser with Optimus Education on their Wellbeing Award for Schools.

Her books include *101 Playground Games 2nd edition* (2021) and *101 Wet Playtime Games and Activities* (2009) and she is a contributing author to *How to be a Peaceful School* (2018).

Thérèse is founder of Thérèse Hoyle Consultancies and creator of the Positive Playtime Academy, where she supports primary schools to significantly improve the quality of playtimes and lunchtimes, with a consequent beneficial impact on wellbeing, learning and behaviour.

She is also a sought-after speaker at conferences nationally and internationally and her work is regularly featured in the media, podcasts and journals.

Thérèse's charity work involves her being on the Board of Directors for the Arbonne Flourish Foundation, supporting the mental health and wellbeing of children and youth for over eight years.

Thérèse tweets at @theresehoyle and @playgroundqueen and can be found at therese@theresehoyle.com and www.theresehoyle.com

Positive Education advocate and former teacher **Frederika Roberts** has extensive experience in supporting the mental health and wellbeing of children and adolescents, staff, and parents/carers through her speaking, training and consultancy work.

She holds an MSc in Applied Positive Psychology and is undertaking a Doctorate in Education with a research focus on whole school wellbeing, based on the model of whole school positive education she developed during her Master's degree.

She is the author of *Recipe for Happiness* (2013) and *For Flourishing's Sake* (2020) and co-author of *Character Toolkit for Teachers* (2018) and the *Character Toolkit Strength Cards* (2020). Frederika is also the founder and Managing Director of 'Educate to Flourish CIC', a social enterprise with a mission to support children's flourishing. Educate to Flourish CIC supports schools in adopting a whole school approach to wellbeing, placing it at the heart of everything they do.

Frederika has presented at Positive Psychology and Education conferences in the UK and worldwide and is a guest lecturer on postgraduate Positive Education modules in the UK, France and Singapore.

Frederika tweets at @frederika_r, @EduFlourish and @FlourishingED and can be found at www.happiness-speaker.co.uk and www.educatetoflourish.org.uk

Bukky Yusuf is a senior leader, science teacher and consultant. She has undertaken a number of leadership roles within mainstream and special school settings, centring around professional development programmes, quality first teaching and learning and effective implementations of Educational Technology. In 2019, Bukky was appointed by the UK Department of Education as co-chair for the EdTech Leadership Group.

As part of her commitment, as a qualified coach, to increase diverse leadership within education, she participates in a number of grassroots educational initiatives and organisations. These include her roles as an ambassador for Leadership Matters, a Network Leader/coach for WomenEd & BAMEEd and a Steering Group member of the #teacher5aday wellbeing initiative. She has run workshops/presentations, on a regional and national basis, that provide practical strategies which help teachers, at all levels, to prioritise their mental health and wellbeing.

Furthermore, Bukky has contributed chapters to a number of books, including *The Early Career Framework Handbook* (2020) by the Chartered College of Teaching, where she provides suggestions to help newly qualified teachers to manage their wellbeing.

Bukky is well known by her Twitter handle @rondelle10_b

ABOUT THE CONTRIBUTORS

Anna Bateman has over 27 years' education experience, including as an inner-city primary teacher, local authority advisor and trainer, and has served on three different governing bodies. She is founder of Halcyon Education, an organisation driven by the opportunity to create a resilient environment in which pupils are empowered to grow academically and personally.

Adele Bates is a Behaviour & Education specialist who supports school leaders and teachers to empower pupils with behavioural needs and SEMH to thrive with their education. She is the author of "*Miss, I Don't Give A Sh*t*" (2021) and a TEDx Speaker 2020. adelebateseducation.co.uk. Twitter @adelebatesZ

Jane Bee has worked in safeguarding for 20 years and provides a consultancy service, training, audits and investigations on any aspect of safeguarding for settings including schools, charities and religious groups. She offers Professional Reflective Supervision for those with a lead in safeguarding within their role. www.janebeesafeguarding.com

Jen Beer (@jennufcboss on Twitter) is a passionate advocate for children's mental health. She uses her BSc in Psychology and Masters in Public Health to apply a research driven and collaborative approach to working with children, young people and families. Jen works in Public Health and has also worked with children's mental health charities.

Sarah Brazenor is a learning coach and has been helping students discover their natural learning ability for the last 10 years. As well as having a BSc(Hons) in Micro-biology, Sarah is a qualified Cognitive Hypnotherapist and NLP practitioner, specialising in learning skills. She believes that everyone can learn but some students need a helping hand.

Matthew Brooker is a Primary School based teacher who has held multiple leadership roles across Kent in the UK. He has a passion and drive to ensure wellbeing is at the forefront of all that he does. He is currently working on a programme which engages children, parents and school staff in furthering their own learning opportunities through Blended Learning.

Maria Brosnan is an Educational Leadership and Wellbeing Specialist with over 30 years' experience; from counselling end-stage cancer patients to whole school wellbeing training. She's the Founder of *Pursuit Wellbeing*, author of *The Pursuit of Sleep* for teachers, and host of the popular educational wellbeing podcast, *Pursuit Wellbeing*.

Founded by psychologist Dr Charles Margerison, and headed up in the UK by **Frances Corcoran** and **Selena Whitehead**, Amazing People Schools is an award-winning learning platform that supports character and wellbeing in schools, drawing inspiration from history's game changers – ordinary people who achieved extraordinary things. Amazing People Schools supports young people to develop their own character strengths and flourish. www.amazingpeopleschools.com

Holly Evans is a 17-year-old student. She plans to study archaeology at university and also hopes to do the Disney Cultural Representative Program. She can be found at @xoholly on Instagram and @hollyjadeevans on TikTok.

Becca Faal is a trained Children's Nurse, Mental Health First Aider and a Protective Behaviours specialist practitioner. She runs Faal Safeguarding, a training and consultancy business, focused on enabling organisations to empower children and adults at risk about safeguarding. She has two MScs in Childhood Anthropology and International Safeguarding.

Anita Kate Garai is a teacher, writer and wellbeing consultant, delivering emotional wellbeing programmes to schools, based on her stories and poems. *Being With Our Feelings: A mindful approach to emotional wellbeing* is a resource comprising four illustrated storybooks and guidebook full of ideas and activities for the whole school community (published by Routledge early 2022) @AnitaKateG anitagarai@hotmail.com

Mark Goodwin has 20 years' experience as a teacher, school leader, trainer and coach. He is the founder of Equal Parts Education – delivering training and coaching to staff and students. Mark's passion is still the classroom and he can be found most days teaching in mainstream, alternative and special. www.equalpartseducation.co.uk Twitter: @MarkGoodwin8

Kelly Hannaghan (@mindworkmatters) puts wellbeing at the heart of education. She is a consultant, motivational speaker, published author and school improvement advisor. Kelly is the founder of the 'Family Matters' empowerment programme. Her work creates outstanding outcomes and awards for schools and organisations. Recognised by the DfE and many leading charities as a lead influencer of mental health and wellbeing in education.

Alison Kriel has a passion for values-led leadership. Following from a 20-year career as a headteacher and CEO she now supports schools nationally and internationally with leadership development, EDI, wellbeing and the unmeasured curriculum. She is the founder of www.aboveandbeyond.education, a safe space for educators and education support services to connect, celebrate, support and share best practice.

Alex Purdie is a Middle Leader in a large comprehensive school in the North West. He is in his tenth year of teaching and has held a variety of roles from Lead Teacher, PSHEE Co-ordinator to his current role of Curriculum Leader of Technology & Food. He is a Professional Mentor, LGBT+ lead, an experienced Primary Governor, a member of the Wellbeing team and proud #HeForShe ally. He is currently undertaking his NPQSL focusing on Parental Engagement and Communication. He tweets on @mrpfoodie

Starting his career as a PE teacher, **Chris Reddy** quickly moved into pastoral leadership and has over 15 years' experience in this area. Chris is the founder and director of Bright Leaders, a social enterprise which 'builds courageous influencers' through delivering leadership coaching and workshops to young people and education professionals. Find him on Twitter @brightleadcoach and @brightleadersuk. www.brightleaders. co.uk

John Rees is a former secondary school leader and led the development of a uniquely effective Health Education programme at Exeter University. Since 2006 he has worked across the UK and overseas to provide coaching and training, aimed at improving the learning and life chances of children and young people. PSHESolutions@gmail.com @PSHESolutions

Dr Sue Roffey has been a teacher, psychologist, academic and author. Currently honorary A/Prof at University College and Western Sydney universities, she is also Director of Growing Great Schools Worldwide. Sue is a prolific author and internationally recognised authority on all aspects of school and student wellbeing. @sueroffey

Ceri Stokes describes herself as 'just a teacher'. She has worked in schools for 25 years, 17 of those in boarding. She has been a Designated Safeguarding Lead for 10 years and is passionate about good PSHE and mental health training. She tweets at @CeriStokes

Stephen Waters has over 40 years' service in education, including 30 as a secondary English teacher and six as a local authority consultant. He is the founder and CEO of the Teach Well Alliance which supports leadership to develop a culture of staff wellbeing and mental health. Stephen is a qualified counsellor, a founding member of the Chartered College of Teaching and an elected member of council.

Elizabeth Wright is an editor, consultant, speaker, and activist, as well as a Paralympic Medallist! She brings forth all of her life experience to challenge people around disability, representation, and inclusion. You can follow Elizabeth on twitter at @esioul

ACKNOWLEDGEMENTS

Any book is a labour of love and this book is more than just 'any' book. It is a book that has galvanised the love of an entire community. This collective love grew this book from the seed of an idea to submission of a completed manuscript in just nine months – no mean feat at the best of times, and this was not written at the best of times.

It is for this love, and all the support, co-operation and sheer hard work that comes with it, that we are immensely grateful to so many people, without whom this book simply wouldn't have been possible.

We would like, first of all, to extend our enormous gratitude to the fantastic community of educators known as the 'Education Wellbeing Collective' – #EdWellColl. The idea sprang from this group's desire to do something that would have a lasting impact on the wellbeing of education communities. It was from this group that we drew most of our contributing authors, who wrote while juggling multiple priorities under exceptionally challenging circumstances.

Of course, an idea for a book is nothing more than that if it isn't written and published. We are, therefore, hugely grateful to every single one of our authors and to everyone who has contributed through being interviewed or completing online questionnaires. The *Big Book of Whole School Wellbeing* simply wouldn't exist without your contributions. Thank you!

We are also immensely grateful to everyone at SAGE Publishing for helping us turn our ideas into reality. We are particularly grateful to our Publisher, James Clark, and to Senior Assistant Editor Diana Alves. From the moment of our first virtual meeting, they understood what this book could and should do, and believed in us and our ability to make it happen – as James said in that first meeting, he could see we were 'women who mean business'! And from that point forward, James and Diana supported us every step of the way, as we bombarded them – and especially Diana – with ceaseless questions, which were always answered promptly and with a smile and warmth that made the entire process so much easier.

A huge, 'thank you' goes out to Andrew Cowley who wrote the Foreword for this book and who, with Thérèse Hoyle, was instrumental in bringing people together in the creation of #EdWellColl.

We would also like to wholeheartedly thank everyone who has taken time out of their busy schedule to read our book proposal to provide a peer review and our manuscript to write an endorsement. These steps are invaluable in getting a book published, then read!

And finally, but by no means least, we would like to issue our heartfelt thanks to our respective families, friends and colleagues for putting up with us not having time for anything other than writing and editing for months on end, and for incessantly talking about our book and our authors. To those who live with us – we know that when we had our editorial meetings on Zoom and you heard us laughing and having lots of fun, it didn't sound much like work, but trust us, we were working! Well, our work and your patience have paid off, because here it is, at last: *The Big Book of Whole School Wellbeing*!

With love,

Bukky   Frederika   Kimberley   Thérèse

FOREWORD

Let us begin with a story … once a primary school teacher, always a primary school teacher.

> Once there was a Tweet. Not one of those Tweets that got lost in the ether as it was ignored by all on the platform, nor one of those Tweets that were sent by those people who seem to be cross at everything and everyone. No; this was one of those Tweets that started a conversation, the kind of conversation where everyone was polite, kind, thoughtful, considerate, empathetic and authentic. The people carried on talking, but decided that they would do more than chat and would do something about what they were discussing.
>
> And they all lived... to write *The Big Book of Whole School Wellbeing*.
>
> The End … of this beginning.

This is not a book about social media. However, social media brought the authors of this project together; like-minded people who have built a bond of professional respect and friendship, who bring a diverse range of skills and insights, passions and interests to the table, alongside a fair dose of the peaks and troughs that their experiences of the education system have given them.

The conversation grew into the *Education Wellbeing Collective* and this volume is the first concrete result of the resolve and resilience of this group.

The initiative for this project was sparked by the pandemic; that invidious, invisible and intrusive invader into all our lives since early in 2020. Pandemics have the potential to change the course of history; they teach us lessons, some of which are followed while others are brushed aside.

If you search for references to wellbeing on a regular basis, read articles, blogs and books and set out to make a difference in your school, this is the book for you. You recognise that children aren't in a good place after a series of lockdowns, that mental health has taken a battering and that 'catch-up' shouldn't be an academic process but a pastoral one, because you know that good pastoral care underpins academic learning.

Schools have changed since the beginning of the pandemic; you will recognise that time away from friends and family, coupled with a fear for the health of loved ones, and being cooped up indoors with a screen for company and a learning schedule met with an unpredictable Wi-Fi connection, has impacted our school communities. You might be looking for some guidance to your thinking. This book will offer you guidance, inspiration and a way forward on the journey ahead.

This book shouldn't sit neatly on a shelf. It needs to be well-thumbed, full of Post-it notes, luminous highlighting and big circles in red biro.

This book delivers what it says on the cover: *The Big Book of Whole School Wellbeing* collates the thoughts of people who have shown a genuine care for their subject, no small level of expertise and a desire to make wellbeing work. Meticulously organised and beautifully written, the text that follows places wellbeing within the context of the culture of the school, recognising that wellbeing should be everywhere, not a bolt-on and certainly not a sticking plaster. Wellbeing through the leadership of the school, through the education of the children, through how, what and when they learn, through engagement and inclusion; wellbeing touches every fibre of our schools. It needs to be lived and breathed, not dismissed as something soft and fluffy.

The *Education Wellbeing Collective* stands for effective and authentic wellbeing in our schools. Wellbeing is for everyday; read the pages that follow and you will appreciate just why.

Andrew Cowley

Former Deputy Headteacher, wellbeing campaigner, blogger and writer, co-founder of 'Healthy Toolkit' and author of *The Wellbeing Toolkit*.

INTRODUCTION

Kimberley Evans, Thérèse Hoyle, Frederika Roberts, Bukky Yusuf

Part I – What is Whole School Wellbeing?

What?

As this is *The Big Book of Whole School Wellbeing*, let's begin by attempting to define 'whole school wellbeing'.

First and foremost, it is a holistic approach, which involves all parts of the school working together and being committed to everyone's social, emotional and mental wellbeing; everyone is considerate and respectful of everyone's needs. The entire school community works with a common goal in mind and everyone is engaged with the ethos and values of the school.

Whole school wellbeing, when done well, seeps into every crevice of the school. It isn't an add-on or a tick-list approach. Wellbeing positively impacts every single stakeholder and, in a true 'whole school' approach, holds equal weighting with learning.

Schools are more than merely places where children go to learn subject content. Schools are places of work for teaching and non-teaching staff, they are where children learn to socialise, form friendships, learn about conflict; they are where children and adults learn to co-exist and compromise. A primary school child will spend approximately half of their waking hours engaged with school and their learning environment, and for an adult that percentage is significantly higher.

Whole school wellbeing therefore requires a systemic approach across the entire school community. That includes wellbeing-focussed policies across all aspects of the school in areas such as homework and marking, email response times and behaviour management, to name but a few. It involves working with the wider school community, supporting parents/carers/families, and the wider community surrounding the school. It entails including wellbeing in initial teacher training and continuing professional development (CPD). It includes teaching wellbeing explicitly and embedding it within the curriculum. These are just some examples of what it truly means to take a whole school approach.

Whole school wellbeing ensures that people are functioning at their best and are able to fulfil their potential. This covers everyone in the school community. We want our pupils to reach their potential in school subjects and have enough energy to engage and excel at activities outside of school. The same goes for teaching and non-teaching staff. We want them to be able to teach and support the school to the best of their abilities and be able to progress in their career, pursue hobbies, excel in other areas and be present for their family and friends.

Why?

On average, children with higher levels of emotional, behavioural, social and school wellbeing have higher levels of academic achievement and are more engaged in school (Morrison and Vorhaus, 2012). A wide body of international evidence points to the positive impact of wellbeing on educational attainment (Adler, 2016; Norrish et al., 2011; White, 2017).

Further evidence points to how pupils' ability to manage emotions can support or impede their learning, their academic engagement, work ethic, commitment and ultimate school success (Durlak et al., 2011).

Additionally, evidence supports the importance of school mental health and wellbeing programmes in underpinning the development of children's social and emotional skills and mental health, and reducing bullying incidences and behaviour challenges (Young Minds, n.d.). This, in turn, has an impact on teaching and non-teaching staff and the school leadership team's wellbeing.

How?

We need to be mindful that, even though we may strive for a collective sense of wellbeing within a school community, what this looks like on an individual basis will differ. Flexible frameworks, robust systems and clearly-defined policies will help to facilitate this on both a whole school and individual basis.

When we are in a position to look after our individual wellbeing, this puts us in a better position to be mindful of the wellbeing of others. In addition, it means we are in a better position to support the school community and to support the wellbeing and progress of students within our schools.

Change is long overdue. Calls for a 'rebalancing' of education have come from teachers, parents and young people (Young Minds, n.d.: 14) and the education community at large (IPEN UKEurope, n.d.). The COVID-19 pandemic has shone a not-so-flattering light on education and has highlighted how, despite many school leaders and teaching and non-teaching staff working very hard to support children's and their own wellbeing, more needs to be done. It now means that we have to support the wellbeing of our school communities in ways we have not done before. Now is a time for change that will serve to benefit the mental health and wellbeing of all.

Part II – About This Book

This book is no ordinary book. It will make you think, it will take you out of your comfort zone, it will inspire discussions around the dinner table and the staffroom kettle and it will instigate great change.

We are confident about all of those things because we have brought together a team of authors who are experts in their respective fields and passionate about creating meaningful, positive change.

At the time of writing, we are living through a unique time, one that no one predicted and one that has caused unprecedented amounts of stress, heartache and pain; it has, however, also brought a welcome opportunity for change. Educators are more acutely aware now of the need for a different type of education system, one that puts wellbeing at the heart of everything, and surrounds all with its protective care.

We also know that it seems like a hill too hard to climb. Where do you start? You might think you are not equipped to do this, that you don't have the training or the expertise. You might have tried and been knocked back.

This book will show you a path forward; it will provide you with tools and strategies that will hold your hand and bolster your belief that you are able to make the change that is so needed.

How to read this book

You choose how to read this book. You can start at the beginning and work your way through to the end. You can dip in and out, finding the parts that are most relevant to you first. You can start with something easy that you already know something about, or you can dive right into the more challenging chapters.

Our authors, who bring a variety of backgrounds and expertise from across the educational landscape, will help you explore a wide range of key aspects of whole school wellbeing.

The book is organised into five sections: *Lead Well*, *Educate Well*, *Learn Well*, *Engage Well*, and *Include Well*. You will notice that the first four sections' chapters all follow the same pattern: The author provides a brief outline of content ('What?'), to allow you to quickly decide whether this is the next chapter you want to read, followed by a rationale for the topic ('Why?'). This is followed by the main section of each chapter, which is the nitty-gritty, the 'How'. Here, each author provides practical tools and strategies for you to consider in your own setting.

More than just reading

Finally, at the end of each chapter ('Over to you'), each author invites you to reflect and make notes, to begin to plan your/your school's next steps in relation to the chapter's topic. Each author provides you with a few questions, steps or reflection points. We invite you to take a few moments to make some notes on these; if, like some members of this editorial team, you have quite the penchant for stationery, this is the perfect excuse to treat yourself to a dedicated notebook to keep all your notes relating to this book in one place. Or, if you are a book scribbler and you are reading this in paperback, go for it and write your notes right here, in the pages of this book.

This is where the magic happens, where you begin to create the positive change you want to see in your school and education at large. So, make sure you don't skip that part. It is, arguably, the most valuable element of this book as the future of education is in all of our collective hands, which means it is in your hands, too.

Include Well

Although this is the last part of the book, we will begin here as this section is slightly different from the others. We pondered and debated whether this needed to be an explicit, separate, section; surely, if the book is about whole school wellbeing, that means everyone within the school community is included? Shouldn't that be implicit and threaded throughout each chapter?

Of course it should, and as you read the book, you will hopefully agree that it is. But as we have seen from the 2020 'Black Lives Matter' movement as just one example, the world is not where we would like it to be just yet. There is much work to be done to be more inclusive and education is no exception. Whether we are talking about race, (dis-)ability, gender, sexuality or any other characteristic, whether protected by law or not, we have come a long way but we still have a long way to go.

Whole school wellbeing is not a 'one size fits all' approach. We have to look more deeply and think about the individual – for pupils and all staff. There may well be sections of your school community that are totally alienated by the wellbeing on offer in your school, not deliberately, but because we haven't yet looked deeply enough at what is offered and how it affects everyone. For this reason, we have decided to dedicate a section of this book to a collection of perspectives on inclusion.

These include a powerful and moving poem by Anita Kate Garai; a hard-hitting, honest perspective from Holly Evans, an adolescent with complex additional needs; experiences of a gay man being out and proud in his school; the many ways in which culture and religion affect wellbeing in ways you may not have thought of; a discussion about how men often struggle to engage with wellbeing; a practical perspective on removing stigma around mental health; and the lived experience of Paralympic triple medallist Elizabeth Wright.

We hope that this final section will sharpen the focus of the entire book and remind us that whole school wellbeing can only be achieved when all members of the school community are included in wellbeing strategies and their practical applications.

Please come to this with an open mind; these contributors are real people with real experiences that are likely to affect someone in your school community. You may not have previously thought that wellbeing affects people in this way, or you may have thought you were doing the right thing, only now to realise that is not the case.

That's OK. Whole school wellbeing is a journey and, wherever you are on that journey, we hope *The Big Book of Whole School Wellbeing* helps you take the first/next step.

With that in mind, then, let's briefly explore each of the sections to help you navigate the book as a whole and choose a starting point for your travels.

Lead Well

In the Lead Well section, we explore how we can lead well and be well as leaders.

Frederika Roberts takes us through the systems and cultures that need to be in place for a whole school approach to wellbeing. She uses real-life examples to explore how schools can implement systems, procedures and school-wide culture changes, and how individuals can take small steps to impact on their own and everyone else's wellbeing. Finally, she invites you to think about your place of work with fresh eyes to see what is already going well and where improvements could be made.

Anna Bateman takes a look at the wellbeing of those who are often so busy looking after everyone else that they forget to look after themselves – school leaders. She takes us through how we can all work together to support each other and why prioritising your own wellbeing is so important.

At the other end of the spectrum, Stephen Waters looks at Early Career Teachers and how supporting their wellbeing should be an intrinsic part of the support they are given. He shares practical ways in which they can be supported, to protect their mental health and retain them within the profession.

Supervision isn't a widely used and understood term in education. Jane Bee and Ceri Stokes explain what it is, the different models available and how it plays a vital role in staff wellbeing, especially for those involved in safeguarding issues.

In her chapter, Bukky Yusuf explores how Educational Technology (EdTech) can support, rather than hinder, wellbeing. She explores the ways EdTech has supported schools throughout the COVID-19 pandemic and invites us to consider the lessons learnt from this so that we can be more connected to each other, communicate better, improve our workflow and reduce our workload, even once we are no longer dealing with the day-to-day impact of a major world event.

Educate Well

The Educate Well section explores various ways that we can support staff (and young people), from individual actions to a whole school stance. It helps us to explore the questions we must ask ourselves, and the systems that are required to facilitate the implementation of answers.

The section starts with practical self-care guidance for busy educators from Maria Brosnan, Kimberley Evans and Thérèse Hoyle. They unpick the terms 'self-care' and 'wellbeing' before outlining the key elements of wellbeing and going on to highlight ways in which educators can transform from a place of surviving to thriving, even when busy.

Jane Bee's chapter takes us through what needs to be in place to safeguard the mental health and wellbeing of staff that undertake Safeguarding roles within a school setting. This is to ensure that Safeguarding team members remain well enough to provide the support for the most vulnerable young people.

Mark Goodwin explores some of the underlying reasons for the behaviours that challenge teachers in the classroom, pointing to (dis-)connection as one of the key factors to consider. He shares how re-creating connections – between teachers and students, between students and school, between teachers and their subject – can allow teachers to focus once again on what is important in school.

In the following chapter, Adele Bates outlines the parallels between the social context a LGBTQ+ person lives within and the effect upon their mental health, even with the law on their side. She clearly explains empathetic ways that school communities can support the mental health and wellbeing of LQBTQ+ young people and staff.

Stephen Waters looks at what can be done to boost the retention of teachers within the profession. His chapter '*The water is draining away – burnout and retention*' identifies the 12 stages of burnout that educators can experience, and the preventative measures – through a five step plan – that schools can implement to avoid this.

In her chapter, Alison Kriel explores how we can address wellbeing in a culture of assessment. With constant tensions between the two, Alison shares her experiences as a former headteacher to outline ways in which the wellbeing of the young people we serve can be maintained alongside rigorous assessment procedures.

Stephen Waters's second chapter within this section considers the role of self-care in retaining Early Career Teachers. He articulates the importance of self-care in the teaching profession and shares its six components to support educators to devise a sustainable self-care plan that fits into their lives.

Learn Well

This section explores ways small adjustments to how we teach, converse and interact with our pupils can have a positive effect on their wellbeing and their learning.

Becca Faal takes us through how to co-produce wellbeing activities with our pupils so they are more relevant and therefore have a greater impact. She explains the true meaning of co-production, then breaks it down into easy steps that you can implement straight away.

Adele Bates shows us how we can learn from the everyday practices of Pupil Referral Units (PRU) and Social, Emotional and Mental Health (SEMH) and Alternative Provision (AP) schools. She discusses the different considerations these learning environments must make when it comes to staff and pupil wellbeing and suggests ways in which their practices could benefit mainstream schools in areas such as safety, teamwork, individuals and relationships.

Mark Goodwin pulls on his experiences with disengaged pupils, and the narratives they use, to explore ways to help pupils fall in love with learning again. Using words that have been said to him over the years, he shares practical ideas and invites us to create the new reality we want to see by making words matter to engage your most unhappy learners.

Frances Corcoran and Selena Whitehead highlight character education in their chapter. They use some great names from history to show how referencing well-known people can support the wellbeing of pupils, staff and the wider school community. They also provide practical steps to embed the development of character strengths into the school day.

Social and Emotional Learning (SEL) has never been more important, but knowing where to start and how to address it properly can be quite daunting. Sue Roffey explains how using the ASPIRE framework can make SEL easier to implement in schools. She provides many practical examples drawn from her work around the world in this area.

Sarah Brazenor explores the emotions around testing and exams – how they can affect a child from a young age all the way to young adulthood, and how we can allay their fears and anxieties. She shows us how to make small, simple changes to the way we talk and interact with pupils that have a huge positive effect.

Engage Well

Sue Roffey provides an overview of the importance of positive relationships as a foundation for wellbeing. She outlines clear, practical ideas to enable us to include and value all stakeholders in creating an open, positive culture across our school communities. There are powerful links in Sue's chapter to the importance of considering circumstances, relationships and emotions in creating a desire for pro-social behaviour, rather than relying on external drivers such as rewards and sanctions.

Kelly Hannaghan highlights the importance of relationships with parents and carers and how crucial their engagement is to the wellbeing and resilience of the entire school community. She breaks down her tried and tested step-by-step approach to achieving purposeful parent engagement.

Kimberley Evans reminds us that staff wellbeing applies to all staff, not just teachers, and that everyone in the school community has a role to play to create positive change. She provides a pragmatic and practical approach to adapting wellbeing strategies and practices so they cater to the needs of different groups of staff and individuals.

One area that is often neglected in wellbeing policies, according to Thérèse Hoyle, is the playground. In her chapter, she sets out a practical, step-by-step approach to ensuring the playground provides a safe and enjoyable environment for children, where they can engage in positive play experiences and enjoyable games. This, she stresses, has positive ramifications across all aspects of school, including teaching, learning and behaviour.

In the final chapter of this section, John Rees takes a closer look at the statutory guidance around relationships, sex and health education in England and how this can be used as a framework to teach these essential topics in educational settings around the world. He warns of the dangers of focusing solely on content and imparting knowledge, and makes practical recommendations for ways we can influence healthy behaviour by creating positive social norms young people will want to adhere to.

Over to you ...

It is now time for you to take the lead. Dive into this book in whichever order and manner works for you, but however you read this book, don't merely read it. Write notes, talk to your colleagues about your reflections, make plans and take action. We have a unique opportunity to change education for the better, and you can play a pivotal role in creating this change. Over to you!

With love,

Kimberley Thérèse Frederika Bukky

Part III – The Education Wellbeing Collective

Thérèse Hoyle

On 12th April 2020 (Easter Sunday) after a Twitter chat with Andrew Cowley and other educators about ways we could support the mental health and wellbeing of children, staff and school communities through the COVID-19 lockdown and beyond, I sent out a message to a community of Educators that read:

> Hi everyone and Happy Easter. I hope you are well and having a good break in the sunshine this Easter weekend. Andrew Cowley and I thought it would be a good idea to put our heads together to think about what schools, teachers, staff and children might need now, during lockdown and when they return to school in terms of support, training, coaching, online courses, education, leadership support, etc. If you'd like to be part of our Education Mastermind, it's this Thursday at 4.30pm, on Zoom. It's an opportunity to put our heads together, support one another, think about the problems and hopefully together come up with potential solutions. If you're in, please join with the link below. Look forward to connecting and if there's anyone I've missed off please forward this to them!
>
> Warmly,
>
> Thérèse

Little did we know that, in just under a year, we'd have written the *Big Book of Whole School Wellbeing* with over twenty authors and built a community of amazing educators, passionate about supporting the wellbeing of staff and pupils through the global COVID-19 pandemic and beyond.

This group still meets virtually every other week with the aim of making a difference in education, and is now called The Education Wellbeing Collective (#EdWellColl).

I am so proud of everyone in our collective, not only for their support of schools, but for the community that has grown – where we have supported each other and cheered each other on throughout this very challenging year.

I am also in awe of our collective's many achievements, starting in the first month with the development of a webpage with a range of free wellbeing resources, blogs, podcasts, worksheets, articles and products for schools. Then, over the summer months, we hosted live panel discussions, where we covered important wellbeing issues such as creating a whole school culture of staff wellbeing, taking responsibility for your own wellbeing, and wellbeing through character strengths. We set up a Facebook group and a Twitter profile to share good practice and ideas and, more recently, a website providing ideas and resources for schools.

In June 2020, in an EdWellColl meeting, a plan was hatched to write a book on whole school wellbeing. We started speaking about chapter ideas and, slowly, a book started to take shape. The editors – Kimberley, Bukky, Frederika and I – then spent many long hours writing a book proposal and approaching publishers. We had one rejection, two offers, came very close to a third offer, and were thrilled go with SAGE Publishing under their Corwin imprint (So, don't ever let a rejection put you off your goals!).

We are thrilled that, throughout this book, we get to share our passion for whole school wellbeing and all we have learnt over our many years of working in education.

Thank you for sharing our journey and welcome to our Education Wellbeing Collective's *Big Book of Whole School Wellbeing*.

With love,

Thérèse

Founder of the Education Wellbeing Collective
To get in touch with the Education Wellbeing Collective please go to:
Facebook: www.facebook.com/EdWellColl/
Twitter: www.twitter.com/EdWellColl
Website: www.edwellcoll.wordpress.com/

References

Adler, A. (2016) 'Teaching well-being increases academic performance: Evidence from Bhutan, Mexico, and Peru.' University of Pennsylvania.

Durlak, J.A., Weissberg, R.P., Dymnicki, A.B., Taylor, R.D. and Schellinger, K.B. (2011) 'The Impact of Enhancing Students' Social and Emotional Learning: A Meta-Analysis of School-Based Universal Interventions.' *Child Development* 82(1): 405–432.

IPEN UKEurope (n.d.) What is Positive Education? Available online at: https://positiveeducation .net (Accessed 1 September 2020).

Morrison, G.L. and Vorhaus, J. (2012) The Impact of Pupil Behaviour and Wellbeing on Educational Outcomes. Available online at: www.gov.uk/government/uploads/system /uploads/attachment_data/file/219638/DFE-RR253.pdf %0A (Accessed 16 February 2021).

Norrish, J., Robinson, J., and Williams, P. (2011) Literature Reviews: Positive Accomplishment. Available online at: www.ggs.vic.edu.au/Positive-Education2/Model-for-Positive-Education (Accessed 3 March 2021).

White, J. (2017) Evidence Summary: Reducing the attainment gap – the role of health and wellbeing interventions in schools. NHS Health Scotland: 21. Available online at: www .healthscotland.scot/media/1693/evidence-summary-reducing-the-attainment-gap-the-role-of -health-and-wellbeing-interventions-in-schools.pdf (Accessed 3 March 2021).

Young Minds (n.d.) Wise Up: Prioritising wellbeing in schools. Available online at: https:// youngminds.org.uk/media/1428/wise-up-prioritising-wellbeing-in-schools.pdf (Accessed 16 February 2021).

SECTION ONE
LEAD WELL

1

CULTURES AND SYSTEMS FOR WHOLE SCHOOL WELLBEING

Frederika Roberts

What?

In order to truly achieve 'whole school' wellbeing, systems and a culture need to be in place that facilitate this. In this chapter, we'll explore the positive impacts on the entire school community when a whole school approach is taken, and the consequences when it goes wrong, before looking at practical examples of how schools are getting it right. Finally, I invite you to consider how you can play a crucial role in achieving a culture of wellbeing in your school.

Why?

Calls abound from around the world for a culture of wellbeing to underpin everything that happens in schools, and to support this with school policies, systems and processes. In her 2018 report, Payne refers to a wide range of benefits to students and staff in 'schools with a positive and communal climate' (Payne, 2018: 1). She cites a positive impact on attendance, engagement and academic achievement and children's socio-emotional health, in addition to a reduction in aggression, substance abuse, school suspensions and expulsions, and criminality. For staff, Payne refers to benefits such as higher job satisfaction and morale, and reduced staff absenteeism. Public Health England (2014) and White (2016) also stress the importance of the school's policies and overall environment, and of instilling a culture of wellbeing in order to best support children's wellbeing and readiness to learn.

A recent impact study carried out at Oxford University (Lindorff, 2020) found evidence, based on research carried out across the globe, of a relationship between wellbeing and academic attainment, with the strongest evidence supporting that a whole school approach to wellbeing can improve academic outcomes:

> There is also strong evidence to suggest that whole-school approaches to promoting wellbeing can have positive effects on a wide range of other student outcomes, including mental health, self-esteem, self-efficacy, motivation, behaviour, and decreased probability of dropout.
>
> (Lindorff, 2020: iii)

For the reasons outlined above, whole school approaches form the basis of most of my work with schools and my academic research. At the core of this lies the understanding that a whole school approach cannot solely focus on children's wellbeing. Much of the training I run in schools centres on providing staff with strategies and a toolkit for their own wellbeing. When writing *For Flourishing's Sake* (Roberts, 2020), I interviewed educators from a wide range of schools worldwide; many stated the crucial role of staff wellbeing:

> Although students are absolutely central and the reason we do what we do, to put them first, you have to have staff in the best possible condition.
>
> Patrick Ottley-O'Connor
>
> In order for my children to flourish, my staff need to flourish.
>
> Dan Morrow
>
> (Roberts, 2020: 33–34)

Cultures and systems for wellbeing need to be driven, or at least supported, by the school's leadership; 65% of respondents to an online survey I circulated in December 2020 stated the school's or Trust's leadership as being ultimately responsible for setting the policy and tone and for facilitating whole school wellbeing.

Simply having a wellbeing policy, or stating that there is a culture of wellbeing, is not enough. In the same online survey, nearly three quarters (73%) of respondents stated they worked, or had previously worked, in a school that simply paid 'lip service' to wellbeing, or had a 'tick list' approach to it.

Examples included

- Being made uncomfortable asking for time off to attend urgent hospital appointments.

- Being told to 'get over' family illness and bereavement during the COVID-19 pandemic.

- In a school where policies and meeting minutes indicated a culture of wellbeing, the headteacher obstructed wellbeing surveys and refused governor requests to hold staff exit interviews.

- A pupil-only focus on wellbeing.

- In one school, staff were not allowed to attend their own children's performances in teaching time. This was demoralising, upsetting and had a huge impact on goodwill.

- Staff were also expected to run school events on evenings, weekends and holidays, which impacted on staff goodwill and affected family relationships.

- Another school had a 'pupil voice' suggestion box, but suggestions were never read nor acted upon, leading to resentment, cynicism and disaffection for any other future programmes or ideas.

According to survey respondents, the consequences of such a superficial approach to wellbeing include

- Exhausted, resentful, demoralised staff who feel undervalued

- High levels of staff sickness (physical and mental health reasons)

- Reduction in the quality of teaching

- Reduction in student engagement

- High staff turnover and loss of experienced staff (it's worth noting that nearly two thirds of respondents stated they *currently* work in a school that has a culture and systems for whole school wellbeing, suggesting that unhappy staff will 'vote with their feet' and move to schools that 'walk the walk' rather than just 'talk the talk').

Whilst the above examples demonstrate the crucial importance of the school's leadership genuinely supporting wellbeing, school leaders cannot do it alone; 60% of respondents to my online survey stated that everyone in school has a role to play.

How?

In my 'LeAF (Learn and Flourish) model of whole school Positive Education' (Roberts, 2019, 2020: 22–23), I highlight 14 elements required to achieve a whole school approach to 'Positive Education', which I describe as equal weight being given to academic outcomes and to student and staff wellbeing and mental health.

Whilst I cannot cover all elements in one chapter, their headings – which range from 'Leadership' to 'Physical Environment' via 'Ethos and Policies' and 'Wellbeing Curriculum' – give some indication of the breadth and depth required of a whole school approach. The overarching themes are reflected in the conversations I have with teachers and school leaders as part of my work as a school wellbeing trainer and consultant, and in the responses I received to the survey I circulated online in December 2020.

The speed of responses I received, on a Christmas holiday evening in the middle of a global pandemic, indicates the importance of whole school wellbeing as a topic of discussion and professional focus around the globe. To give the responses more context: Just over half (55%) of respondents were teachers, one third were in senior leadership or headship roles, 5% held wellbeing roles, and the remaining respondents were split equally between governors, non-teaching staff and union representation. The majority of respondents (70%) were in England, 13% in the United Arab Emirates, 5% in Scotland, with the remaining respondents split equally between China, New Zealand, the Republic of Ireland, Wales and Switzerland.

Key takeaways were that clear policies and systems are required to make wellbeing a genuine focus within school, that consistency is important, and that whilst some of the little extras such as free lunches, massages and other staff wellbeing initiatives can be great, these cannot be applied as the only interventions and need to be tailored to staff needs. It is also important to note that 'staff' does not mean only teaching staff; in Chapter 21, Kimberley Evans helps you explore how to consider the needs of non-teaching staff as part of a whole school approach to wellbeing.

Pupil wellbeing was mentioned the least in responses to my survey, though there were great examples such as 'young wellbeing ambassadors', one-to-one pupil coaching and a bespoke wellbeing toolkit for certain year groups.

Perhaps the main focus of responses was on staff wellbeing because, as one respondent indicated, many initiatives for children's wellbeing exist in schools, whereas staff wellbeing still requires much work. This is reflected in the findings of the 2020 Teacher Wellbeing Index (Education Support, 2020): Pressures on education professionals' wellbeing and mental health have led to over half (52% of all education professionals, 59% of senior leaders) considering a change of profession, with high workload being cited as the main reason by over three quarters (76%) of senior leaders and over two thirds (68%) of education professionals overall.

Policies

Most of the responses mentioned the importance of having policies with a staff wellbeing focus, particularly around marking, emails, and time for 'planning, preparation and assessment' (PPA).

Marking policies

Rachel Poulton, a member of the senior leadership team in a school in the United Arab Emirates, said her school has a digital feedback policy allowing for verbal, rather than written, marking. Senior leaders and teachers from schools in England also referred to marking policies designed with teacher workload in mind.

When I interviewed Flora Barton (now Cooper) for *For Flourishing's Sake,* she described how, when she began her headship at Crowmarsh Gifford Primary School in Oxfordshire, England, she set out to ensure all staff could 'leave at least twice a week at 4.15pm with nothing in their hands' (Roberts, 2020: 37).

Five years after she introduced this policy, one of Flora's teachers had embedded verbal feedback in lessons so successfully that he had done no marking at home for nearly three years.

Emails and other communications

A number of schools have introduced email and out of hours communications policies. One school in London, England, for example, has a policy of 'no emails before 8am or after 4pm on workdays'. Rebecca K, a senior leader, told me that her school has a staff email protocol which sets out 'reasonable expectations for email responses'. Another teacher referred to an 'email curfew', a term also used by Jo Owens, Director of Ethical Leadership at Lichfield Cathedral School:

> Because of the school's organic growth, the school has a quirky structure spread out across several buildings [...]. This [...] resulted in staff sending and receiving many internal emails. The school's leadership team therefore made a decision to set an e-mail curfew between 7pm and 7am, legitimizing staff not to respond to e-mails immediately. This has made a big difference in giving staff permission to go home and stop working in the evenings. Key to the effectiveness of this policy has been the effort by members of the senior leadership team not to email staff during the curfew hours. If people do send an e-mail after curfew, it's either a mistake or an emergency, so this is rare.
>
> (Roberts, 2020: 37–38)

PPA time

Although it is a legal requirement for most teachers in England and Wales (National Education Union, 2019) to be given PPA time of at least 10% of teaching time, the amount and structuring of PPA time seem to differ greatly between schools. This featured significantly in my survey responses, with respondents valuing schools that allow teachers to take occasional PPA time at home, for example.

Time off and breaks

Policies allowing staff to take time off during school hours to attend their own children's school events, guaranteed lunch breaks and staff wellbeing days were other examples of policies aimed at supporting staff wellbeing.

Training

Jessica Austin-Burdett, Head of Art, Design and Technology in a school in England, values that her school's CPD is 'subject needs-based', while Heidi Groesche, a teacher at an international school in the United Arab Emirates, likes that her school provides training that goes beyond teachers' 'technical development'.

A number of schools invest in external providers to support staff wellbeing. Miss G, a senior leader in an English school, told me her school has wellbeing staff briefings and has hired an external wellbeing provider to support staff. Dr Victoria Carr, Head-teacher at Woodlands Primary School, also in England, told me:

… we buy into the concept of resilience training by buying in a range of trainers to support resilience in staff.

Mentoring and coaching

This was mentioned by a number of respondents to my survey. One teacher told me their school has a trained mental health mentor for children and staff, others talked about regular 'check-ins' with staff, and another told me that their school has invested in coaching and a wellbeing award.

Peer support

A number of teachers told me their schools have trained mental health first aiders, while one respondent mentioned trained mental health 'ambassadors'. One school has a system where staff 'buddy-up' with a colleague in a different department so they can openly share any concerns and support each other.

Behaviour

Behaviour is a topic close to my heart, as the stress this caused ultimately drove me out of the teaching profession. According to the Teacher Wellbeing Index, in October 2020, 84% of education professionals (89% of senior leaders) described themselves as stressed (Education Support, 2020).

A number of respondents to my online survey who described their schools as taking a whole school approach to wellbeing mentioned that this included behaviour policies specifically designed with staff wellbeing in mind.

What can you, as an individual, do?

As stated earlier, the responsibility for creating a culture of and systems for whole school wellbeing, while needing to be driven and supported by the school's leadership, rests with everyone; that means you.

First of all, you need to take responsibility for your own wellbeing, managing your mental and physical health in all the ways you have control over; from nutrition, to sleep, to self-care practices, there is much you can do to look after your own wellbeing. This is covered in more detail in *Self-care for busy educators – a practical guide* (Chapter 6). If you want to explore the area of self-care even further, I recommend *Teacher Wellbeing & Self-Care* (Bethune and Kell, 2021).

Additionally, consider the following (the list is by no means exhaustive)

- Be kind (to others and to yourself).

- If your school has policies to support your wellbeing, follow them (e.g. don't respond to parent emails late at night – unless it is an emergency).

- Consider volunteering for peer support roles.

- Seek help if you're struggling.

Over to you

We have merely scratched the surface of a huge topic in this chapter. Hopefully, however, the examples above have given you food for thought. Now take some time to make notes on how you can personally contribute to a culture of whole school wellbeing in your school.

- What is your school already doing well?
- How could it improve?
- What steps will you take to make this possible?
- Whose support can you enlist?

References

Bethune, A. and Kell, E. (2021) *Teacher Wellbeing & Self-Care*. London and Thousand Oaks, CA: Corwin.

Education Support (2020) Teacher Wellbeing Index 2020. Available online at: www .educationsupport.org.uk/sites/default/files/teacher_wellbeing_index_2020.pdf (Accessed 1 March 2021).

Lindorff, A. (2020) The impact of promoting student wellbeing on student academic and non-academic outcomes: An analysis of the evidence. Available online at: https://oxfordimpact. oup.com/wp-content/uploads/2020/10/Wellbeing-Impact-Study-Report.pdf (Accessed 3 March 2021).

National Education Union (2019) Workload and working time. Available online at: https://neu .org.uk/advice/workload-and-working-time (Accessed 30 December 2020).

Payne, A.A. (2018) Creating and sustaining a positive and communal school climate: Contemporary research, present obstacles, and future directions. Washington, DC. Available online at: www.ncjrs.gov/pdffiles1/nij/250209.pdf (Accessed 31 March 2021).

Public Health England (2014) The link between pupil health and wellbeing and attainment. Available online at: https://assets.publishing.service.gov.uk/government/uploads/system/ uploads/attachment_data/file/370686/HT_briefing_layoutvFINALvii.pdf (Accessed 30 March 2021).

Roberts, F. (2019) 'LeAF: The Learn and Flourish Model and Self-Evaluation Framework for Whole School Positive Education.' Unpublished manuscript, Anglia Ruskin University.

Roberts, F. (2020) *For Flourishing's Sake: Using Positive Education to Support Character Development and Well-Being*. London and Philadelphia, PA: Jessica Kingsley Publishers.

White, M.A. (2016) 'Why won't it Stick? Positive Psychology and Positive Education.' *Psychology of Well-Being* 6(2).

2

SELF-CARE FOR LEADERS — LOOKING AFTER YOUR MENTAL HEALTH

Anna Bateman

What?

If you've ever been on a mental health training session within education, you will often find that the wellbeing and mental health of leaders is mentioned at the end. I'm guilty of doing this many a time. But why is it an afterthought or an add-on? By the very nature of the profession, everything in school is quite rightly geared towards pupils; from progress and curriculum to safeguarding and wellbeing. However, in October 2020, an online survey (Education Support, 2020) stated that 89% of senior leaders described themselves as stressed. Having worked with senior leaders for many years, this data doesn't surprise me, nor will it be a surprise to senior leaders themselves, rather a confirmation of something they know already. With a shrug and some resignation, leaders I work with know that their job is stressful, and that this is part of the position they hold. So, is there an unreasonableness in expecting things to be different? It is not necessarily a case of either/or but that working in a stressful environment and self-care can and should co-exist. This chapter outlines how to raise the importance of a proactive stance to senior leader self-care and wellbeing within a stressful environment.

Why?

For too long, senior leaders' mental wellbeing and self-care has been ignored, and sadly this continues to be reinforced currently by a lack of governmental policy and guidance for placing the wellbeing of senior leaders at the heart of school improvement. Whilst huge strides have been made in the last few years to improve the wellbeing of teachers, senior leaders are not mentioned in any statutory guidance. For example, the updated Ofsted framework (2019) – Ofsted is the Office for Standards in Education, Children's Services and Skills in England – makes strong references to teacher wellbeing, placing the onus on leaders to achieve this, without referencing the wellbeing of the leaders themselves. The Department for Education recruitment and retention strategy (DfE, 2019) in England also shows that there is a movement to retain staff and that workload is currently the biggest challenge to staff wellbeing. According to the latest Teacher Wellbeing Index (Education Support, 2020), poor mental health is believed to cost the UK education sector, and consequently the public purse, £1.1bn–1.5bn per year. Furthermore, according to research by the Health and Safety Executive (HSE, 2020), the education sector ranks amongst the highest in Britain for work-related stress, depression and anxiety.

There remains however, guidance within the Governors' Handbook (DfE, 2020) that governing boards should have due regard for the wellbeing and mental health of the school leadership team and teaching staff more broadly.

What is really important to acknowledge is that the leadership team sets the tone for the rest of the school, particularly in relation to mental health and self-care. This was also reflected in the responses to Frederika Roberts's survey (see Chapter 1).

Sometimes for example, when there is an absence of a commitment to staff wellbeing and self-care within the leadership team, you might start to see the competitive, 'badges of honour' culture that is particularly unhealthy. A member of staff is sitting for lunch and another member of staff might say 'you've got time for lunch – oh good for you, I don't even have time for a drink'. This has the potential to create guilt and a level of shame for the member of staff who has decided that they need a lunch break in order for them to look after their wellbeing and feel refreshed enough to teach well during the afternoon. This competitive culture of who is busier, who's not had sleep, and coming into school even when ill, is an extremely unhealthy environment. Is it acceptable that a culture of competitiveness over who is the busiest/most stressed/tired/ill is OK? Is it something which is encouraged as a solution to maintaining a high performance or high accountability culture?

The other challenge is, of course, that if the senior leadership team does not attend to their own wellbeing, they face long-term consequences: the impact of stress includes life-limiting illness such as heart attack, stroke or cancer and life-challenging conditions; for example, increased risk of heart disease, memory loss, weight gain, chronic fatigue syndrome, depression and anxiety-related disorders, as well as digestive and sleep problems. These are the very serious impacts of not including staff wellbeing and self-care as an essential part of a whole school approach. The job is stressful, and that is not likely to change soon, but the impact of stress can be limited with a commitment to caring for our health and that of those in our team.

In the absence of governmental guidance, how can we begin to address the issue of the mental health of senior leaders?

How?

'Walking into the Wind' is a phrase that well-known education leader Steve Munby has used to describe school leadership and developing resilience (Munby, 2014). You may want to read about his approach to leadership further in his book *Imperfect Leadership* (Munby, 2019); it's a perfect way to describe what leadership in schools is like. When we walk into the wind, our eyes are stinging, face and body is buffeted and essentially, we feel like we are getting nowhere. If you have been 'walking into the wind' for a while, you would begin to arm yourself with a decent coat, shoes, or even a face covering. You may start to get used to the buffeting and might start to understand which days seem worse than others. You may also begin to ask others to walk with you, so that you can share the buffeting and take it in turns to be at the front.

Let's take this idea of the individual response/resilience to the wind, buying a coat and shoes for example. What does that individual response or responsibility look like for you?

Well, I'm fairly sure that you wouldn't decide not to wear a decent coat or shoes for six weeks and then wrap up for the week that the wind has died down, but this is what happens when we decide to only carry out the activities which help our wellbeing and stress levels during the school holidays. Our individual responsibility is to ensure that we commit to a regular dose of activities that help us to feel well. This list of activities could be extensive and will range from creativity, reading or sport and physical activities, to being with others, to wanting to be on your own. Perhaps use the opportunity now to reflect on what is essential to you. What do you do that makes a difference to your life and you can't be without?

So, what about the idea that some days are better than others? Another part of our commitment to self-care is the self-awareness of knowing our strengths and challenges. Are there certain aspects of how you lead which are more challenging than others? For example, when there is a significant change or life event happening in your life, does it affect your ability to remain resilient? If so, how can you plan for this? Can you be proactive about the support you might need? There is a fantastic free resource from Robertson Cooper called the 'iResilience survey' (Robertson Cooper, n.d.). After you answer some key questions, it gives you a report on your own resilience and where your areas of challenge or strengths might be.

So, what about the team? The people who walk with you on a windy day and share the buffeting? I'm sure that, on your leadership journey, you have learnt lots on team dynamics and building a team, so I'm not going to cover this. However, having a school governor who is responsible for wellbeing and has a strong focus on the senior leadership team (SLT) is essential. Hold a meeting with them and ask them to help the SLT maintain a level of focus on self-care.

Ensure the team has good knowledge and training about mental health and how to spot the signs of stress and burnout, so that you can support one another. Endeavour to create a culture where staff can safely say when they are not OK. One senior leader

I worked alongside had a policy that any member of the senior leadership team could come and talk to them any time they were overwhelmed and needed support, even if it was just to plonk themselves onto a chair and vent or sit quietly. The member of staff was never shamed for this and was provided with check-ins and ongoing support following the chat if needed. As a result, the school was and felt like a caring place to work, where staff retention was reasonably high and pupil progress was outstanding.

Finally, it is also helpful to have a good Human Resources person at your disposal, so that you can provide support and enable wellbeing activities that align to current government and local authority guidance.

Whole school culture

As I have alluded to right at the beginning of this chapter, the school culture can set the tone for good wellbeing or can create a culture of toxicity – and senior leaders set the tone. One of the ways that can help create and maintain a good self-care culture is a staff wellbeing policy that has been co-produced with staff, senior leaders and governors. This policy will set out the key objectives, values, systems and processes that will ensure the wellbeing of every member of staff is valued, alongside the challenges that come with working in a stressful environment.

What has been interesting, having worked in hundreds of schools over the last ten years or more, is that for some schools, the one-off wellbeing events such as yoga, secret buddy or a pizza during a staff meeting have had a benefit. However, for the majority of schools the longer-term type activities such as an enforced leaving at 4pm every Friday, no expected email replies at the weekend or an improved feedback and marking policy, have had a big impact.

This further establishes the need therefore for a bespoke policy that meets the needs of your school and your staff. The policy alone won't establish the safe, self-care environment; a drip, drip, drip approach of key clear messages that the wellbeing of all staff is essential will be what makes the difference.

You can read more about the systems and cultures for whole school wellbeing in Chapter 1.

Over to You

Use Table 2.1 to reflect on your own wellbeing and self-care and the self-care of your team. Take a 'best fit' approach by checking in the box next to each statement. Red would indicate that this activity is not in place or hasn't happened yet.

(Continued)

Where there is partial completion of the activity or action, this would be amber; and finally, green would indicate that this activity is already in place and embedded into practice.

Table 2.1 Audit tool of self-care and the self-care of your team

	Red	Amber	Green	Notes:
You are committed to regularly taking time to de-stress				
You have a clear idea on what helps you maintain good wellbeing out of school				
You regularly participate in that activity, at least weekly				
You have a good understanding of the impact that stress plays in our long-term physical and mental health				
You have a strong support network of people around you				
Is there a governor responsible for mental health and wellbeing, who takes an active role in senior leadership wellbeing?				
The senior leadership team have had training on adult mental health and wellbeing				
Your senior leadership team often feel able to discuss when they are having a tricky day				
There is a staff wellbeing policy in place which has been developed with staff				
The staff wellbeing policy outlines the whole school culture, processes and systems which are in place to support and develop good self-care				

References

DfE (2019) *Teacher Recruitment and Retention Strategy*. London: Crown Publishing. Available online at: https://assets.publishing.service.gov.uk/government/uploads/system/uploads/attachment_data/file/786856/DFE_Teacher_Retention_Strategy_Report.pdf (Accessed 28 March 2021).

DfE (2020) *Governors' Handbook: For governors in maintained schools, academies and free schools*. London: Crown Publishing. Available online at: https://assets.publishing.service.gov.uk/government/uploads/system/uploads/attachment_data/file/270398/Governors-Handbook-January-2014.pdf (Accessed 28 March 2021).

Education Support (2020) Teacher Wellbeing Index 2020. Available online at: www.educationsupport.org.uk/resources/research-reports/teacher-wellbeing-index-2020 (Accessed 23 February 2021).

HSE (2020) Work-related stress, depression or anxiety statistics in Great Britain. Available online at: www.hse.gov.uk/statistics/causdis/stress.pdf (Accessed 5 March 2021).

Munby, S. (2014) Resilience – 'Walk into the wind'. 22 August. Available online at: https://vimeo.com/104073649 (Accessed 30 March 2021).

Munby, S. (2019) *Imperfect Leadership: A book for leaders who know they don't know it all*. Camarthen and Willington, VT: Crown House Publishing.

Ofsted (2019) The Education Inspection Framework. Available online at: www.gov.uk/government/publications/education-inspection-framework (Accessed 5 March 2021).

Robertson Cooper (n.d.) iResilience. Available online at: www.robertsoncooper.com/iresilience/ (Accessed 23 February 2021).

3

THE ROLE OF LEADERSHIP IN RETAINING EARLY CAREER TEACHERS

Stephen Waters

What?

The importance of investing in the professional development of Early Career Teachers (ECTs) was acknowledged by the UK government's introduction of the Early Career Framework (DfE, 2019a) effective in England from September 2021. It was, in large part, prompted by the worrying number of ECTs leaving the profession. Attrition data also needs to be seen against the backdrop of the challenges of recruiting graduates to the teaching profession.

This chapter evaluates the effectiveness of the Early Career Framework (ECF) in its aims to increase retention and improve recruitment. School leadership is pivotal in achieving the aims of the ECF and the school leader's role in this regard is examined in detail. While staff wellbeing and mental health is not included in the ECF, there is a compelling case that it must underpin the delivery of the ECF for the framework to be effective. While taking care of mental health is particularly relevant for ECTs, developing a whole school culture of staff wellbeing is also critical for staff retention and supporting recruitment of all staff. While this chapter is set within the context of the ECF for England, the principles apply to the support of ECTs everywhere.

Why?

The data on recruitment and retention

According to the 2018 school workforce census in England (DfE, 2018), one in six teachers (15.3%) who qualified in 2017 left the state school sector within a year, the highest figure for more than 20 years. One in four teachers left within three years and 33.3% within five years. The impact on individual schools, as well as on the teaching profession as a whole, is considerable:

- Staff morale is affected, making it more likely that other ECTs will resign. Many ECTs leave because their wellbeing and mental health has been damaged and some suffer burnout (more about burnout in Chapter 10). In some schools, bullying has also contributed to, or is mainly responsible for, ECTs suffering from mental ill-health.

- If vacancies are difficult to fill or remain empty, lack of continuity of staffing affects the classes covered by supply staff or teachers on short-term contracts. This is especially true if a number of supply staff cover classes – for example, if a temporary or permanent teacher cannot be recruited.

- The innovation, enthusiasm and drive that ECTs often bring with them is lost. Schools need this 'new blood' to stimulate their growth and development and to bring energy and fresh ideas into the school.

The aims of the Early Career Framework

The early career teacher framework extends the period of support for newly qualified teachers (NQTs) to two years, with a dedicated mentor, funded training and professional development, including access to online resources. ECTs are assessed against the Teachers' Standards (DfE, 2011), which focus on the five core areas of behaviour management, pedagogy, curriculum, assessment and professional behaviours, and build on Initial Teacher Training. There is no reference to wellbeing and mental health in the ECF, other than obliquely in relation to workload:

> ...assessment can become onerous and have a disproportionate impact on workload.

> (Early Career Framework, DfE, 2019a: 20)

This is a serious omission that can only be addressed by school leaders. However, it is worth noting that it is likely that leaders themselves lack training in staff mental health. The National Professional Qualifications (NPQs), from middle to executive leadership, do not cover how to implement a culture of staff wellbeing and mental health in schools.

The DfE Teacher Recruitment and Retention Strategy (DfE, 2019b) speaks of the importance of school leaders developing a school culture in which workload is made more manageable. But although workload is important, as we will argue in Chapter 12, it is only part of the picture.

In Walker et al.'s (2018) report, NQTs spoke of the importance of a whole school culture where induction was viewed as the start of a lifelong journey of training and support. Recently Qualified Teachers (RQTs) – those that have passed the NQT phase of training – also commented that a key reason for them staying in their settings was because of the positive and supportive school culture. We argue that this culture should include a commitment to staff wellbeing and mental health, not just for NQTs and RQTs, but for all staff.

In England, the Office for Standards in Education, Children's Services and Skills (Ofsted) is responsible for ensuring that organisations that provide education, training or care meet the required standards. For the first time, the 2019 update to the Ofsted inspection framework (Ofsted, 2019a) and school inspection handbook (Ofsted, 2019b) set out expectations of school leaders in relation to workload, wellbeing, bullying and harassment. To be rated as 'outstanding,' leadership and management would have to engage with staff at all levels and deal with issues, including workload, 'appropriately and quickly' and staff would report 'high levels of support for wellbeing issues' (Ofsted, 2019b: 74).

To achieve a 'Good' grade, leadership is required to 'take account of the main pressures' on staff and be 'realistic and constructive in the way they manage staff, including their workload' (Ofsted, 2019b: 74). Leaders also 'protect staff from bullying and harassment' (Ofsted, 2019b: 75).

The Ofsted framework (Ofsted, 2019a) and inspection handbook (Ofsted, 2019b) raise important questions for school leaders in relation to support for ECTs:

1. How do 'leaders engage with their staff'? The verb 'engage' is intended to have positive connotations in the criteria, although engagement can also be negative or counter-productive. What mechanisms are in place to engage ECTs? Anonymous surveys? Focus groups? Via feedback from Middle Leaders' meetings? 'Door always open' policy?

2. How do leaders 'take account of the main pressures' on ECTs? This suggests that leaders are not only aware of the pressures, but take action to reduce them. How does leadership know the pressures ECTs face? How much of this pressure is caused by external forces and how much by internal leadership and management? What does leadership do to reduce the pressures?

3. How do leaders show that they are both 'realistic and constructive' in how they manage ECTs and their workload? Do leaders know how many hours ECTs are working each week? Do they encourage and support a work-life balance? Are they aware of circumstances beyond the school gates which may affect how individual ECTs are able to manage their workload?

4. Sadly, there are too many teachers reporting incidents of bullying in the workplace. How does the school ensure that ECTs are protected from bullying and harassment? What mechanisms are in place for ECTs to report incidents? What happens to the bullies? Is there a different reaction when pupils are being bullied? If so, why?

How?

Key leadership actions to support ECTs

We will now look at some of the key leadership actions that can support ECTs. Walker et al. speak of the 'practice shock' (Walker et al., 2018: 8, 19, 54, 75) when NQTs begin to teach, and advise that they need help to acclimatise to the reality of work in schools. Alongside their formal mentor, we suggest partnering an NQT with a teacher who has recently qualified, to share strategies for coping with the transition from Initial Teacher Training (ITT) to practising teacher. Coaching is gaining momentum as a strategy to provide support, enabling teachers to cope with the emotional demands made on them and to develop professionally. Coaching equips staff in schools to find their own answers to challenges, while providing them with a supportive non-judgemental relationship.

Leadership should reduce, or preferably replace, high-stakes judgement-led account-ability with professional development, organised and documented by the staff. ECTs can be paired – or form groups of three – to carry out Lesson Studies, instead of conducting judgemental observations, where professional discussion identifies successes and challenges of teaching and learning and shares classroom practice to receive supportive feedback which is confidential to the participants.

Remove learning walks, unless they are supportive. Most teachers find unannounced visits of leadership to their lessons unhelpful, unless their purpose is to monitor pupil behaviour and to ask the teacher if they need any support. ECTs especially find 'drop-ins' stressful.

Create a buddy system for ECTs. Buddies support one another, for example they bring their buddy a drink when they are on break duty; they are there to listen when times are tough; they share strategies for managing their workload; they are there to support when lessons don't go well. Enable ECTs to attend their own children's key life events, e.g. nativity plays and graduations. Review and reduce ECT workload. Ask 'What impact does this strategy or action have on staff wellbeing and mental health?' When introducing an initiative, ask the same question. If the answer is that it decreases staff wellbeing, modify or reject.

Give as much control to ECTs for decision-making as you can and increase their professional autonomy. Trust them to do the right thing, rather than micromanaging them to prevent them doing the wrong thing:

> Trust comes from being part of a culture or organization with a common set of values and beliefs. Trust is maintained when the values and beliefs are actively managed.
>
> (Sinek, 2011: 178)

Perhaps more than experienced staff, ECTs need to feel that they are part of something bigger than themselves and that they are making a difference to the lives of the pupils they teach. Belonging to a school community with a well understood set of values prevents isolation. This became even more important during the COVID-19 pandemic which led to social distancing from colleagues and a lack of face-to-face contact with pupils and staff.

A weekly 'shout out' where staff nominate colleagues for doing something which improves staff wellbeing is not only motivational but it emphasises the importance of individual contributions to a shared goal. Sinek (2011) warns of the consequences for organisations if motivated employees do not feel part of a common purpose:

> Unless you give motivated people something to believe in, something bigger than their job to work toward, they will motivate themselves to find a new job ...

(Sinek, 2011: 152)

Perhaps this is one of the reasons why the number of ECTs leaving the profession is so high:

> 32.3% of newly qualified entrants in 2016 were not recorded as working in the state sector five years later. This is the highest five-year wastage rate on the current series, which dates back to 1997. The rate has been between 25.4% and 32.3% in each year over this period.

(Foster, 2019: 3)

Thank your ECTs and show them appreciation, privately and publicly. A 'Thank you' costs nothing but is priceless. If someone has something to shout about, ask them to do the shouting themselves, for example in a staff briefing. Support them and give them the confidence to do so.

Form a staff wellbeing group and include ECTs. Timetable meetings at a time when the school is already meeting within directed time, e.g. a staff meeting. Give ECTs permission to talk about their mental health with their mentor. Talk about your own mental health and the challenges you face as a leader. This reassures ECTs that they are not alone. Survey ECTs anonymously each term to get feedback on their wellbeing and mental health. Adjust support where necessary.

Move away from an expectation that pupils' work is pen-marked to a default of verbal feedback. Staff can still be given the discretion to pen-mark from time-to-time, if they wish. Create an email policy which limits receipt of emails to the working day, e.g., emails to be sent between 08.00–17.00. Incorporate a scheduler into your email system. ECTs can then draft an email to be sent at an appropriate time. This is one example where technology can support wellbeing in schools; Bukky Yusuf explores this area further in Chapter 5.

Create a system for staff to be able to discuss their mental health and wellbeing concerns confidentially. This could be internally with the wellbeing lead or a coach, for example, or externally with a counsellor, by buying into an Employee Assistance Programme.

Your overall vision is to build a system-wide culture of staff wellbeing and mental health within which ECTs are supported, both emotionally and practically, in relation to their workload. Your aim is to look after your staff so that they can teach more effectively and have the capacity to take care of the children. Unsurprisingly, what is good for ECTs is also beneficial for all staff.

Over to you

Building this culture takes time: not less than 12 months, in the first instance, with Years 2 and 3 incorporated into the school improvement development plan:

Step 1: Form a staff wellbeing group, including ECTs, and/or appoint a wellbeing and mental health lead.

Step 2: Survey ECTs anonymously every term to find out what is helping and what is hindering their wellbeing and mental health.

Step 3: Ask the staff wellbeing group to review the survey results and make recommendations to SLT for how support for ECTs could be improved.

Step 4: SLT review the recommendations and create a 12-month action plan to implement as many as possible, ranking them in the order in which they will have most benefit to ECTs' wellbeing.

Step 5: Implement strategies.

Step 6: Include impact of actions in the termly survey.

Step 7: Evaluate at the end of 12 months.

Step 8: Include vision and aims in Years 2 and 3 of the School Improvement/ Development Plan.

Step 9: Celebrate successes with the staff.

Step 10: Repeat during the next 12 months.

In Chapter 12, the importance of ECTs taking care of themselves is discussed.

References

DfE (2011) *Teachers' Standards*. London: Crown Publishing. Available online at: www.gov.uk/government/publications/teachers-standards (Accessed 28 March 2021).

DfE (2018) *School Workforce in England*. Available online at: www.gov.uk/government/statistics/school-workforce-in-england-november-2018 (Accessed 5 March 2021).

DfE (2019a) *Early Career Framework*. London: Crown Publications. Available online at: https://assets.publishing.service.gov.uk/government/uploads/system/uploads/attachment_data/file/913646/Early-Career_Framework.pdf (Accessed 5 March 2021).

DfE (2019b) *Teacher Recruitment and Retention Strategy*. Available online at: www.gov.uk/government/publications/teacher-recruitment-and-retention-strategy. (Accessed 5 March 2021).

Foster, D. (2019) 'Teacher recruitment and retention in England' (2019) Briefing Paper Number 7222. 16 December 2019. House of Commons Library.

Ofsted (2019a) *The Education Inspection Framework* (EIF). Available online at: www.gov.uk/government/publications/education-inspection-framework (Accessed 5 March 2021).

Ofsted (2019b) *School Inspection Handbook: Handbook for inspecting schools in England under section 5 of the Education Act 2005*. Manchester: Crown Publishing. Available online at: https://assets.publishing.service.gov.uk/government/uploads/system/uploads/attachment_data/file/884310/School_inspection_handbook_-_section_5.pdf (Accessed 28 March 2021).

Sinek, S. (2011) *Start With Why: How great leaders inspire everyone to take action*. London: Penguin.

Walker, M., Straw, S., Worth, J. and Grayson, H. (2018) *Early Career CPD: Exploratory research. National Foundation for Educational Research*. London, Department for Education. Available online at: https://assets.publishing.service.gov.uk/government/uploads/system/uploads/attachment_data/file/916492/Early_career_CPD-exploratory_research.pdf (Accessed 28 March 2021).

4

STAFF SAFEGUARDING AND SUPERVISION — LESSONS FROM COVID-19 AND BEYOND

Jane Bee and Ceri Stokes

What?

This chapter is intended to help those that are about to consider safeguarding supervision for staff wellbeing. Based on the journey a Designated Safeguarding Lead (DSL) took when considering what she wanted from supervision, and the experiences of an expert who has helped schools implement the changes, we will look at what professional supervision is, the different models available and what they mean for a DSL.

From the perspective of someone providing professional supervision, this chapter will explore the importance of having somewhere completely safe to air concerns and feelings about the impact safeguarding work can have on those undertaking it. We will highlight, with examples from our own practice, some of the challenges and benefits of implementing a supervision model before taking a broader look at some of the available models and sharing our top tips for school leaders and for safeguarding staff.

Why?

The September 2020 Keeping Children Safe in Education (KCSiE) statutory guidance for schools and colleges in England (DfE, 2020) was initially put out for consultation with the possibility that supervision would be compulsory for those working in safeguarding. This sent ripples out across the education world, as many staff did not really know what supervision meant; we already had (and understood) line managing, mentoring, counselling and coaching. How could supervision fit in? And would this be just another tick-box exercise that was supposed to help with staff wellbeing, like compulsory yoga or bonding sessions? After all of this, the KCSiE that was published for Sept 2020 had a noticeable gap: Supervision was off the cards. The reason seemed unclear, although many local authorities stated that safeguarding staff had enough to deal with, without implementing something new, and that it would be in 'KCSiE 2021'. Instead of something that was designed to help, this implied that supervision would be something extra that the safeguarding team needed to include to support their staff; this added to the feeling of overwhelming confusion.

So perhaps we need to take a step back and ask what 'supervision' actually is and how it can benefit staff wellbeing?

Often DSLs advise that they would like to have time to reflect on their own practice, to talk to someone about how a situation has made them feel and what effect it has had on their subsequent practice. In reality, this is difficult within a school setting; time for reflection often gets lost or is used up by more pressing matters. Despite being busy, we need to guard against this and ensure that those in a safeguarding role have their needs met. Supervision is vitally important to reduce a dip in wellbeing and an increase in anxiety, sickness and burnout. Professional supervision can also provide a safe place to discuss issues which are not easy to address in school, such as how a DSL is managed, or how they offload information and stress if they are a DSL who is also the headteacher. Professional supervision is therefore a useful tool that plays an important role for DSLs.

Professional supervision supports you personally by involving an impartial third party. This helps you reflect on your own feelings, thoughts, behaviour and general approach within the workplace and provides you with a completely safe space to do so. It can help to reflect on practices, explore new ideas, look at other ways to solve problems, help with decision-making and, in turn, increase motivation in the workplace.

If you are well supported personally by your professional supervision, it follows that this will also support you in your professional role. In a nutshell, professional supervision provides you with:

- An agreed framework for discussing challenging situations that arise in any aspect of life, but always bringing you back to how this affects you in the workplace.

- Protected time to consider and discuss complex problems.

- Greater confidence, leading to better working practices.

How?

How can we find supervision for our ourselves and staff especially when there are so many options out there? It is concerning that the starting point is often the wrong question:

'What would inspectors be looking for as evidence of supervision?'

DSLs can feel swamped with meeting inspection criteria, new jargon and more acronyms. The idea that staff sign a contract before starting supervision can feel overwhelming. Many DSLs have tried coaching, but this is more focused on career development; some recommend mindfulness for staff wellbeing, but this is a personal support system and perhaps does not fit into the school structure. Is supervision another fad – a fad that schools will feel frustrated to have to invest more time and money into?

As with most new initiatives, there is a lot to take in. Much reflection into how you can implement these policies and procedures into school, and consideration of how your staff will respond to the new initiative, are required. Reading and research around this can help build confidence to ask questions, so when the Local Authority advice comes out, you will have clear questions to take to the Headteacher and Senior Leadership Team (SLT). Questions such as:

- How/who it will be delivered or received by?
- Do all staff need supervision?
- Can a line manager give supervision?
- Can a support member of staff receive supervision?

Every school is different and one size does not fit all, but it is key that the SLT all buy into the chosen model and see the benefits. Many DSLs will struggle to really understand how they can fit it into an already busy day. As a typical teacher, they will ultimately keep going back to the question:

'How would this benefit the child?'

Looking at this in this way, a DSL may realise there are many layers to supervision:

- A chance to review good and bad practice in a non-judgmental environment.
- A way to improve practice and outcomes.

- A chance to share good practice and boost staff confidence in dealing with challenging situations.

- A way to help share the burden and therefore help with staff welfare.

This can seem overwhelming, but many schools already have great supervision; they just do not call it that and do not record it as such. As a starting point, it could be useful to discuss this during safeguarding audits and with HR teams. Time is an obstacle for many schools and the temptation to drop supervision as the academic year gets busy will be high. Staff need to feel invested in the process to prevent this.

In order to answer some of these questions and explore some of the layers, it might be useful to look at some models of supervision and explore which fits best for you.

Peer supervision

This can work well with a group of DSLs or headteacher but can also cause problems because it might not be a safe space in which to raise issues. You might open yourself up and share things, then the next day find yourself in a meeting with the same people. However, if you opt for this route, find a small group of four–six people, an uninterrupted room, and set yourself a time and date. Put a written agreement in place regarding confidentiality, support and being non-judgemental, and set an agenda. This will help you ensure that the time is used equitably. Most importantly, ensure the 'same place same time' element so there is continuity to your arrangement.

Cyclical model

The cyclical model was first published in 1994 and adapted by Page and Wosket (2014). We like this model because it involves:

- contract – terms agreed between the supervisor and the supervisee

- focus – what the work is going to be about and how each session will look

- space – reflective, exploratory, and developmental (building session on session) work that takes place throughout the process of supervision

- bridge – the way supervision sessions allow the supervisee to bring what has been worked on back to the workplace (bridging the two)

- review – an opportunity to re-contract and talk about the supervisory relationship, i.e. what is working well, what is lacking and what needs re-formulating.

4x4x4 model of reflective supervision

The 4x4x4 model of reflective supervision (Wonnacott, 2012) was originally written for social work supervision and suggests that there are four stakeholders in supervision:

- service users (i.e. pupils in a school)
- staff
- the organisation
- any partner organisations.

There are four functions of supervision in this model:

- management – of work and cases
- development – of the individual and their work
- support – for the individual, recognising the emotionally demanding work
- mediation – the relationship between the supervisor and supervisee.

And the final x4 are the elements of the supervisory cycle itself which covers:

- experience of the individual
- reflection on what has gone well and not so well
- analysis of what might be done better
- putting this into action in the workplace.

In this model, all the components are interdependent, so it is a dynamic style of supervision, promoting reflective practice, critical thinking and clear decision making.

Seven-eyed supervisory model

Hawkins and Shohet (2012) developed the seven-eyed supervisory model, which looks at the interactions between client, therapist and supervisor in its various – direct or indirect – combinations. While this is a complex model, there are some aspects that can be useful for DSLs and in education. The model has an educative aspect, which looks at the emotional response to your work, and a systemic aspect, so it is able to zoom in and out from the very detailed aspects of your work to a much wider look at systems. What sometimes looks like an issue in your working practice might actually be a systemic issue. An example of this happened when someone receiving supervision was becoming frustrated with the reporting of safeguarding issues and things getting missed. Supervisor and supervisee firstly focused on the aspects of missed detail, but when they 'zoomed out', they realised there was a much wider systems issue.

Whichever model you choose, and there are far more than listed here, the principles of supervision are to provide you with a safe space in which to 'bring all of who you are at work' in order to ensure you can do the very best in safeguarding for whoever you work with – so in the case of a teacher, for the children in your school.

Key elements to successful supervision

The space must be confidential. It's a safe place to talk about your team, managers, home, relationships, cases etc, but the supervisor will always bring you back to 'how are you at work?'

You need a set time and date – it may seem strange but we know how busy you are and things will slip – like your 1:1s – and most importantly you will need a contract. The purpose of the contract is to keep bringing you back to what you've agreed as your priorities, no matter what you're talking about. So, for example, something going on at home is completely appropriate to discuss, but the supervisor will always bring you back to 'how is this affecting your ability to do your job?'

Supervision should be reflective, with the supervisor actively listening and using thoughtful questioning, helping the supervisee to consider all aspects and to guide but not make decisions for the supervisee.

Coaching or supervision?

Often the question of difference between coaching and supervision arises. The difference is really the focus. Supervision has a focus of upholding standards and managing resources: 'How are you and how does this relate to your role?' It looks to the past in order to look to the future and supports staff to download what has been happening, so they don't carry anything that is not theirs; it creates safety for the professional as well as the child and family. Coaching, on the other hand, is about looking forward, and focuses on the personal and professional development of the person. They are different approaches, but clearly there is an overlap.

Top tips for school leadership

- Do some reading and keep reflecting.

- Decide as a school what supervision means to you.

- Define, with staff who are having supervision, what it is and what the benefits are.

- Do not feel that you have to start afresh and make big changes.

- Do not beat yourself up about not achieving perfection.

- Before deciding on professional supervision;

  - Take some time to think about what you want from professional supervision

  - Find someone you like and who has experience

  - Check what model they are using – does this fit with what you want or how you feel your thoughts are ordered?

  - Take time to discuss the contract – important to get this right

  - Decide on times and frequency that fits with you and your role.

- Never cancel supervision.

- Persevere until session 5 – before this, you are still finding your feet and developing a supervisory relationship, but if it doesn't feel right by session 5, stop the agreement, as it probably isn't right for you.

Over to you

- What outcome are you aiming to achieve from the introduction of safeguarding supervision?
- How will you know if safeguarding supervision is effective for the individual and for their practice in school – how are you measuring the impact?

References

DfE (2020) *Keeping Children Safe in Education.* Available online at: www.gov.uk/government/publications/keeping-children-safe-in-education–2 (Accessed 5 March 2021).

Hawkins, P. and Shohet, R. (2012) *Supervision in the Helping Professions.* Maidenhead: Open University Press.

Page, S. and Wosket, V. (2014) *Supervising the Counsellor and Psychotherapist* (3rd Edition). London: Routledge.

Wonnacott, J. (2012) *Mastering Social Work Supervision.* London: Jessica Kingsley Publishing.

5

HOW EdTech CAN HELP SCHOOLS MAINTAIN INDIVIDUAL AND COLLECTIVE WELLBEING

Bukky Yusuf

What?

The year 2020 was the year that saw a global and astronomical rise in the use of technology, more specifically the use of Educational Technology (EdTech) while distance learning was undertaken. This experience demonstrated something that many thought was impossible through this particular platform – EdTech could help educators to maintain connections, working relationships and interact in ways that aided wellbeing.

This chapter will review – through the lenses of connection, communication, workflow and workload – the ways in which our social interactions alongside mental health and wellbeing, can be enhanced through the use of EdTech, and consider what needs to be put in place to facilitate this. I will use examples of how my own school used EdTech to maintain our individual/collective wellbeing, and to highlight how simply and effectively it can be done. This is not only in the case of blended learning, self-isolation or any other constraints imposed upon us to control the spread of disease. This can also help to revolutionise connections with staff that work on a flexible basis and who are not always on the school site for the whole of a working week.

Why?

A number of articles (Curnock Cook, 2019; Fullbrook, 2021; Parker, 2017) look at how EdTech can aid the mental health and wellbeing of our students, but there is little regarding its use to support the wellbeing of the staff that teach them.

Recent events have clearly demonstrated how easily uncertainty can give rise to anxiety. Yet, during the most uncertain times, the role of a leader/manager remains the same: to support your team members/staff. This includes supporting their mental health. That said, during these periods, it is common to witness how often communication channels close and connection opportunities diminish.

Technology can provide an effective means of establishing, maintaining and sustaining school-wide connections that make us feel part of the school community, thereby enhancing our sense of wellbeing. Lessons learnt from lockdown are therefore pivotal in this regard, as being off-site is no longer a deterrent for the business of school to continue. Let's consider it another way: snow days will now be transformed forever.

Yet, how can school leaders prevent isolation from work affecting our individual and collective wellbeing? Living in a digital era means that technology will always be a part of our professional and private lives.

This chapter will help school leaders put systems in place to ensure that wellbeing considerations are placed alongside the desired outcomes of technological tools that are being deployed.

How?

School policies relating to the use of technology can be written in a way that supports, rather than hinders, wellbeing.

Let's take a look at some examples through the lenses of connections, communications, workflow and workload.

Connections

Positive social relationships have a significant impact on wellbeing and the overall culture of a school, as Sue Roffey explains in Chapter 19.

When you connect with staff through the technological platform of your choice, how do you check in with them to see how they are? To find out how things have been? To learn of what may have happened since you last spoke? An understanding of these will help to frame formal meetings in appropriate ways. It will also help you to understand why staff members may not be engaging as expected.

Without these questions at the forefront of your mind, it can be easy to slip into the mindset of 'business as usual'. A deliberate focus on checking-in will help leaders to quickly recognise when someone is experiencing difficulties. A recent study conducted by Mind Share Partners with Qualtrics and SAP (Greenwood and Krol, 2020) found that nearly 40% of employees worldwide revealed that they hadn't been asked by anyone at their company whether they were OK. There was also 38% more likelihood of this group reporting their mental health had worsened during the COVID-19 pandemic. Beyond the pandemic, this highlights the necessity to ask remote working staff how they actually are.

Since virtual communications inadvertently convert our 3D real life nuances into a 2D experience where the communication subtleties are lost, additional efforts are required to make up for what is being 'lost in transmission'. Aggregating this additional effort across a day/week/month can drain energy levels and, in turn, affect our sense of wellbeing.

We therefore need to ensure that our connections and modes of communication are timely, effective and purposeful.

If you were to review the EdTech you have within your school, what would it uncover? What do you already have? How well can staff use it? What training is in place to ensure that staff can use it well? How well do the platforms aid workflow and avoid duplication of information?

What do your EdTech platforms need to be used for? How clearly has this vision and understanding been shared with all relevant stakeholders and staff members?

How will the technology be used to communicate with staff on a whole school, leadership team, department, small group, or one-to-one basis?

Informal discussions behind the scenes can help in reaching key school-wide decisions.

However, what do you have in place to avoid everyone's emails being jammed up with messages that are not relevant to them or which quickly become out of date once they have been acted upon?

Free messaging services are examples of tools that can be used to aid communication in terms of immediacy, informality and ease of document transmission. These can also facilitate quick updates and celebratory news. Note, however, that safeguarding and GDPR practices still need to be implemented even for information that is being shared in more casual ways.

When it came to meetings, 2020 demonstrated how efficiently these could be run in a virtual setting. Let's look at it another way: for many schools, it highlighted how much time was generally wasted during face-to-face meetings – time lost in covering and discussing items that could have easily been shared within an email – or, more importantly, in the recognition that meetings were not always required. You know, the meeting for the sake of a meeting …

Generally, meetings are a key way to establish and cement connections at different levels across a school setting. Technology can help to make the meetings more efficient/timely and free people up to spend time on more important tasks. In order to achieve this, leaders need a consistent focus to streamline whole school/department/one-to-one meetings by asking questions such as:

- Who needs to be present in the meeting?

- What's in place for staff working on a part-time or flexi basis?

- How easily can the meeting be accessed remotely?

- Which tools can be used to capture the minutes/everyone's contributions to the discussions?

Not every meeting needs to have formal minutes captured. If it is a meeting to collate ideas and views, digital platforms such as JamBoard or Padlet can allow multiple participants to contribute their ideas simultaneously in writing and/or through images which can then be stored and retrieved. It can help to maintain the sense of group working/community-building, even if this is done on a remote basis. Remote working does not mean that working relationships have to be remote. Part of the meeting should also build in time to check how everyone is.

Communications

One source of frustration for part-time/flexi staff can be the realisation that dates for school events have been shared in their absence, yet the expectation is that they will be aware of them and fulfill required actions. This is something that can be simply avoided by effectively using the calendar feature included on many platforms. You can use calendars to update school events across the school year, which can then be accessed by all staff as and when convenient. Some platforms allow you to send email notification reminders and advance notice of forthcoming events to reduce the worry about forgetting anything important. This is a straightforward way to help everyone feel part of the school community and avoids the feeling that you're only in the loop if you happen to be in the right place at the right time.

Workflow

Another source of frustration for teaching staff is the inefficient planning/sharing of teaching resources and curriculum materials, finding yourself working in isolation with multiple versions and feeling that you are reinventing the wheel.

Staff will generally make any workflow issues they experience known. This can provide a golden opportunity to do things in a different and smarter way.

When you consider these issues, what technological solutions do you have in place that can help to diminish them?

For example, is there any way in which resources can be shared that:

- reduces the use/print out of paper

- avoids the duplication of work

- allows relevant staff to access the same document and collaborate?

Workload

Workload can mean different things to different people. Put simply, workload means

'the amount of work or of working time expected or assigned' (Merriam-Webster, n.d.).

We live in an era where we are all time poor and there never seems to be enough time to do what needs to be done, so it is vital to recognise whether staff are given enough time to complete tasks. Here are some key questions to help us prioritise what should be done:

- What are staff being asked to do? Why?

- How does it contribute to the progress students are expected to make? If it is not contributing to the progress of students, it comes lower down in the list of priorities or could be scrapped altogether.

- When it is necessary to undertake these tasks, which aspects are repetition? Can these be automated?

- Which aspects are taking a lot of time? Can 'shortcuts' be used to reduce the amount of time?

- Are staff trained well enough to use the most effective techniques, thereby reducing time? Feeling skilled/having the confidence and competence to effectively carry out a role can aid the wellbeing of an individual.

Over to you

My vision with regards to EdTech is to ensure that it supports the continuity of face-to-face working relationships within a virtual forum. With careful and strategic consideration, this vehicle can maintain the sense of community, thereby aiding our sense of purpose, job satisfaction and therefore our individual/collective wellbeing. We now live in a digital era, so technology is here to stay and can have an important role in our lives as we adopt new ways of working within a school context.

What's your vision? Make some notes below.

- What is your vision to support the mental health and wellbeing of your staff?
- How could this be implemented in an online setting?

(Continued)

- What do you need to have in place, remotely, to aid this implementation?
- Which type of communications/connections do they facilitate? Video? Text? Audio?
- Which technological platforms do you have within your school that can increase workflow/reduce workload?
- How often do you audit/survey the needs of staff?
- How do you know what's required?

References

Curnock Cook, M. (2019) Can Edtech help with student wellbeing and mental health? Available online at: www.hepi.ac.uk/2019/11/05/can-edtech-help-with-student-wellbeing-and-mental-health/ (Accessed 30 March 2021).

Fullbrook, K. (2021) 7 ways to improve school wellbeing through EdTech. Available online at: www.innovatemyschool.com/ideas/7-ways-to-improve-school-wellbeing-through-edtech (Accessed 30 March 2021).

Greenwood, K. and Krol, N. (2020) Crisis Management: 8 Ways Managers Can Support Employees' Mental Health. *Harvard Business Review.* Available online at: https://hbr.org/2020/08/8-ways-managers-can-support-employees-mental-health (Accessed 30 March 2021).

Merriam-Webster (n.d.) workload. Available online at: www.merriam-webster.com/dictionary/workload (Accessed 30 March 2021).

Parker, R. (2017) How edtech can boost good mental health. Available online at: www.innovatemyschool.com/ideas/how-to-use-edtech-to-boost-good-mental-health (Accessed 30 March 2021).

SECTION TWO

EDUCATE WELL

6

SELF-CARE FOR BUSY EDUCATORS — A PRACTICAL GUIDE

Maria Brosnan, Kimberley Evans and Thérèse Hoyle

What?

The terms 'self-care' and 'wellbeing' are often misused, misunderstood or overused to the point of being meaningless. They can send us running for the hills because they're synonymous with a tokenistic approach to our health, often requiring us to do things we don't want to do 'for our own good'.

In this chapter we'll demystify self-care and help you understand why it's vital. We'll define some key terms to make it a little less onerous and a lot more accessible. We'll share a five-step framework to help empower you in your personal and professional life. We'll also look at how we inadvertently damage our own wellbeing with poor habits, not addressing problems or trying to be all things to all people.

Self-care starts with you, but doesn't mean doing everything for yourself, by yourself. It doesn't mean other people don't have responsibilities, too. Being responsible and proactive for your self-care would ideally go hand in hand with your school doing their utmost for your wellbeing, too (see also Chapter 10 by Steve Waters). When they work in synergy, you flourish. If not, it can feel like you're barely surviving.

All this in just one chapter? Absolutely. Hold on to your hat, it might be a bumpy ride.

Why?

Wellbeing is defined by two key factors; how you feel and how you function in the world. When we feel good, we tend to function well. We're better teachers, leaders, friends or parents. But when we're stressed, anxious, overwhelmed or exhausted, all of these things suffer. The consequences of not taking care of ourselves are serious and can have a negative impact on our relationships and our lives.

According to the *Teacher Wellbeing Index 2020* (Education Support, 2020), the wellbeing of UK education professionals is consistently lower than that of the general population. The same report revealed:

- 84% of education professionals described themselves as stressed.

- An increase in symptoms of poor wellbeing, such as much higher levels of depression (32%) than the general population (19%).

- Large increases in symptoms such as:

    o difficulty concentrating;

    o insomnia;

    o tearfulness.

These are all symptoms indicating a lack of self-care.

Take a moment to reflect – have you experienced any of them? How often? Maybe you need to connect the dots to realise that that is why you're feeling the way you are. It might help to re-read that list and think again.

Ultimately it's our personal responsibility to take care of ourselves.

In our busy lives as educators we are so busy looking after everyone else that we tend to forget to look after ourselves. One of the metaphors we feel is most misused is the oxygen mask analogy. You know the one, we've all heard it: you need to put your oxygen mask on first so you can help others. Why is it that helping others is the key thing here? We firmly believe that kindness matters, but why are we drumming home the message that you only look after yourself so you can look after others? How about, we look after ourselves simply because we matter. You matter, your mental and physical health and wellbeing matter. Put yourself first simply because you deserve to thrive, flourish and be happy.

You could probably list a number of friends and colleagues experiencing these kinds of symptoms without recognising that they apply to you as well. We race through life in a state of stress and don't realise the issues that are accumulating. Sometimes it is easier to ignore what is happening to us rather than deal with it. We take on an attitude of 'I can't deal with that right now' and push it away, stick our head in the sand. Especially when we don't know where to start. Even if we recognise an issue, it can be overwhelming to know what to do about it and we push it away again. But we ignore these things at our peril, and there can be dire consequences to our physical, mental and emotional health.

Because self-care is down to us, it is all too easy to ignore. We are rarely on the top of our priority list. Actually, are you on your list at all? Look at your to-do list, amongst all the jobs around the house, work deadlines and things you are doing for others, is there anything on there that brings you joy?

It's time to take care of you, for you; it's time for you to flourish.

How?

We've designed a five-step plan to get you started, which we will now outline:

Step 1: What are you tolerating?

Every day we lose time and energy unnecessarily because we're putting off or tolerating things that we shouldn't. We sweep things under the carpet that we end up tripping over.

- Wincing with tooth pain when eating but not making time to go to the dentist.
- Grimacing in the mirror because you haven't managed to get to the hairdressers.
- Stressing over the state of your finances, but not spending time sorting them out.
- Picking that towel up off the floor (again!) because there's no towel rail.
- Avoiding people at parties because you didn't remember their birthday or say thank you for a gift.
- Incurring penalties because you haven't paid your bills.

The list can go on. We become like leaky sieves, promising ourselves that one day we'll sort these things out, but not making time. You might think these things don't affect your wellbeing, but the nagging feelings go on draining your energy and taking away from the very areas you'd like to spend time on.

Where in your life are you wasting time and energy on thoughts, actions and procrastinations? What are you putting up with in your life? What are you tolerating in:

- Your house
- Your wardrobe

- Your physical appearance

- Your work environment

- Your professional relationships

- Your health

- Your finances

- Your paperwork

- Your personal relationships

- Your future?

Write your list and plan to eliminate whatever is holding you back from flourishing.

Step 2: Creating delicious daily habits

Healthy habits make our lives run more smoothly and support us to incorporate healthy behaviours. You've probably heard that it takes about thirty days to create a new habit, so give yourself time to embed these new habits into your life – don't give up too soon. Habits that replenish us and make us feel good send a strong message that we care for and value ourselves. Create a list of five things you would like to do on a regular basis. These are not things you feel you should do, they're things that you want to do and bring you joy. Write down what you will do:

Each day try to do at least one or two of these. You are forming a habit of being loving to the central most important part of your life – you.

Here are some ideas to get you started, but make sure they work for you and bring you joy:

- Go for a run

- Lose yourself in a project

- Watch a sport

- Watch your favourite TV programme

- Read for pleasure

- Prepare a delicious meal

- Lie in the beautiful sunshine

- Go to bed early

- Listen to relaxing music with a cup of tea
- Journal
- Give yourself a five-minute foot massage.

Step 3: Healthy boundaries

Boundaries are rules that we communicate to others about what we will or will not accept. Boundaries protect us and keep us safe.

They define what is important to us, where our priorities lie, and how we'd like to be treated. When used well, they create a healthy, mutually respectful framework for relationships, both at work and at home.

- Start small. Practise saying no to small things regularly, to build your boundary-setting muscle.

- Take time to respond before saying yes. Some phrases like 'Can I come back to you?', 'I can't do it this week, but I can do it next week', 'What should I drop if I take this on?' can really help.

- Establish a proper structure to your day, including making time for lunch and a set time to disconnect from work.

Healthy boundaries work best when everyone is working together as a team and understands what a healthy boundary actually is.

Step 4: Healthy communication

One of the most important things in school is good communication. It leads to better relationships and healthy wellbeing. When we communicate effectively and we're more open about what we are trying to achieve, it gives people the opportunity to be more understanding and empathetic to our needs. People aren't mind readers but we often expect them to be. We get cross when they don't make allowances for our needs, but if we don't communicate well with them, how can they understand? See also Chapter 5, by Bukky Yusuf, for ways to use technology to support wellbeing through effective communication.

Here are a few examples:

- I need to take a break from my screen every hour otherwise I get a migraine.
- I need to pick up my child by 4pm.

- I want to be more efficient at marking, please remind me of this if I'm procrastinating.

- Working late in the evening will affect my sleep, could we have a morning meeting instead?

Step 5: Healthy flexibility

One of the keys to healthy wellbeing is being confident enough to embrace flexibility. Every term is different in education, so think about how you can adapt your wellbeing goals and priorities at different times throughout the year and empower yourself to adjust them accordingly.

What will work in the summer months may be difficult to achieve in the dark winter months for example. You may need to let things go at certain times of the year, or double down and focus on them more to help you deal with seasonal stresses.

- Going for a run may be easier in the summer months than the winter; do you need an indoor activity for the winter?

- Use your diary well to acknowledge there are busy times of the term and be careful not to overload those times with other things.

- Having a bath may be the ultimate luxury in the depths of winter, but in the middle of a heatwave you may need to think of another way to treat yourself.

- Your capacity can be different throughout the term; what you can take on in week 2 is very different from what you can take on in week 10.

We are all affected by natural cycles; the changes of the seasons and rhythms of the day, the month, the year. The more we can honour these and learn how our lives are affected by them, the better it is for our wellbeing. For instance, women may like to consider how they can adapt their goals and working practices to match their energy levels in their menstrual cycle. For more on this we can highly recommend Red School (n.d.).

Only you know what works best for you, as it is a very personal thing. Above all, be kind to yourself and flexible when it is needed for you.

Over to you

One of the best ways to embrace self-care is to set achievable goals. We only have 24 hours in a day; think about what you can realistically achieve. But also think: are you using your time effectively? Making small tweaks in your day can make huge positive changes to your life.

(Continued)

If you are a seasoned pro at prioritising your own wellbeing, how could you take it further? Sometimes we rest on our laurels and think we are doing as much as we can, but life or our skills have moved on and we could actually do more for ourselves.

- If we waved a 'realistic magic wand' over your wellbeing in the next 3-6 months, what would it look like?
- What small actions could you start today, to help you achieve this?

References

Education Support (2020) Teacher Wellbeing Index 2020. Available online at: www .educationsupport.org.uk/sites/default/files/teacher_wellbeing_index_2020.pdf (Accessed 3 March 2021).

Red School (n.d.) Red School (website). Available online at www.redschool.net/ (Accessed 27 March 2021).

7

WELLBEING AND SAFEGUARDING

Jane Bee

What?

This chapter aims to highlight the importance of wellbeing within safeguarding. Keeping children safe, both by taking preventative measures and by acting on immediate concerns, is hugely rewarding, but those of you who work as the Designated Safeguarding Lead (DSL) or as part of the safeguarding team within school will also know how emotionally stressful this is and how mental health and wellbeing play a part.

In England, government guidance on safeguarding for schools (DfE, 2020) has formally recognised the mental wellbeing aspect of safeguarding and amended the definition of safeguarding to include both physical and now mental health of children and young people. This means schools must take action to promote the welfare of pupils who are suffering or likely to suffer significant harm and also must take any changes in the mental wellbeing of pupils as an additional indicator of potential abuse.

This chapter will look at how schools might do this, while also looking at how we ensure that the mental wellbeing for staff, particularly those working in the safeguarding team, is supported, and that they remain in a good enough wellbeing headspace to enable them to support those children who are our most vulnerable.

Why?

Children who are abused and staff working to prevent this, or to take action if it has already happened, are a part of the school community who need particular care.

Imagine a scenario where a child already known to the school to be vulnerable has been sexually abused at home and, in addition to the obvious physical distress, whose mental wellbeing is suffering as a consequence. Perhaps they are fearful of being alone with staff or showing signs of extreme tiredness because they are too frightened to fall asleep at home, or they are wearing the same clothes because they don't want to get undressed at all, including for physical education (PE). Now imagine a member of staff who is anxious about deadlines, performance and workload and who, because of this, sees the actions of the child as poor behaviour; they have deliberately missed a planned one-to-one meeting, or deliberately not brought in PE kit and have stayed up all night playing computer games. How might we increase the wellbeing of the child so that they feel safe to make a disclosure in school, and how might we enable the member of staff to create that opportunity by having enough in their reserve wellbeing tank to think contextually about what might be happening and take the time to do so?

Each school should be recognising who their most vulnerable pupils are and should be ensuring that there is a particular focus on their wellbeing. However, pupils will only be protected if we also support staff with their own wellbeing and ensure they are able to take a step away from their daily stressors and pick up on wellbeing indicators from pupils.

In turn, when a safeguarding issue has been recognised and reported to safeguarding staff in school, without enough in their own wellbeing reserves, we risk potential breakdown in resilience and therefore their own wellbeing, often, in my experience, leading to burnout and sickness. Many DSLs feel they are 'fire-fighting'. By this they mean only dealing with high risk situations which require immediate action rather than being able to put safe systems in place and to support staff in enabling the wellbeing of pupils who are showing the less obvious signs of abuse.

Improving the wellbeing of our safeguarding staff means that they will be in a better place to support other staff who, in turn, can support pupils. This cascade of wellbeing becomes a culture which serves to protect the school's most vulnerable pupils in a way that means abuse is recognised faster and children are better protected.

How?

For me, there are four main links between safeguarding and wellbeing. The first is that we know from experience that children often show mental health difficulties or unusual behaviour when they are experiencing trauma at home. Children who are physically or sexually abused will also experience an element of emotional abuse, as will children who are severely neglected. This might include fear, anger, violence, abuse of others, smearing (or regression in toileting and hygiene), or a deliberate change in appearance, e.g. eating disorders or self-harm. Emotional abuse is also a stand-alone category; for example, children living in a household where there is domestic abuse are at risk of significant harm from emotional abuse, even if they themselves are not physically harmed.

The second main link is our own mental wellbeing. Can we really be in a place where we can pick up on the behaviour of children who might be suffering from trauma, if our own mental wellbeing isn't at a reasonable level? As staff in a busy school there are always so many other things to consider, and our wellbeing reserves are often at rock bottom.

Thirdly, when I'm working in schools, I'm always struck by the resilience of those working in safeguarding and the amount of emotionally difficult cases that come their way from a variety of different sources, often outside of the school. I have seen first-hand, however, that resilience is only there until suddenly it isn't. There is little warning and burnout is real. We must look after our own mental wellbeing if we are to recognise trauma in children and young people while also supporting other agencies (such as children's social care), staff who have referred a concern to us and might themselves feel anxious, and parents who may be devastated to learn of abuse or who may themselves be going through a prosecution. As has been suggested by Steginus (2019), when we expend too much energy and don't invest enough energy back into ourselves, we experience burnout. Stephen Waters explores burnout for school staff in more detail in Chapter 10.

The fourth is the mental wellbeing of parents or family members who care for children and interact with the school on their behalf. Are they clear on the effects that their own behaviour might be having on the mental wellbeing of their children and family and are they in a mindset which enables them to listen if this is recognised? Do they know how to recognise the difference between normal childhood behavioural changes and a mental wellbeing deficit in their own child and are they in a position to react accordingly?

So, if a child is being abused and showing signs of trauma, and parents and school staff don't recognise this due to their own mental wellbeing not being in the right place, or the DSL is unable to work efficiently due to burnout, you can see how these four might interact to form the perfect storm. In the worst case scenario, a child showing all the signs of being abused will not receive the help he or she needs.

Practically, there are some things we can put in place within school to help. Let's look at the school's culture. Are staff supportive of each other and are they encouraged to be? Sometimes a culture of toxic positivity can creep in because we don't have the time or energy to listen and support. Lukin (2019) writes that we are increasingly encouraged to focus on positives and to reject anything which involves a negative response in us. However, by doing this, we are also increasingly moving away from difficult aspects of our lives and this can have a consequence on our wellbeing and simply cause us to stop sharing our concerns. In the world of safeguarding this has the opposite effect to what is desired. For example, someone going through a difficult time might be told about someone going through an even more difficult time, or advised to 'put it out of their minds', or that things will 'work out'. But how is this helpful? A better response would be to state how you hear the person, how you understand that this is a difficult time and to offer support. A positive culture within the staff room and around the school can greatly assist staff in giving and receiving support, which has the effect of increasing wellbeing. Talking to staff about this and beginning the change in thinking is a positive step forward.

Another practical step is to aim to support mental wellbeing issues for parents. Schools that do this well are the ones who make it as easy as possible for parents to seek help for themselves or for their child. In Chapter 20, Kelly Hannaghan explains her step-by-step process for purposeful parent engagement, and how this has supported the mental health and wellbeing of the children and families she has worked with.

I was once at a school parents' evening where it was clear that a parent was agitated and anxious, constantly looking at the door and checking her watch. The child, too, was anxious and jumpy, pulling at his mother's clothes and clearly wanting to leave. Instead of asking whether everything was ok and giving the parent the opportunity to talk, the teacher doggedly ploughed on through the child's progress report and moved on to the next parent. Later it became apparent that this was a serious domestic abuse situation and that the woman's partner was waiting outside. He had threatened violence if she took too long. The teacher was unable to recognise this because she herself was stressed and working against the clock. Her own worries were left unsupported in school and she was not in a position mentally where she was 'listening'. The child was therefore placed at further risk of significant harm. While not the fault of the teacher, often meetings can start off as one thing but become safeguarding like this example; you haven't factored in the time for this, the energy for speaking to parents about something different, perhaps referring to children's social care and ultimately the time to support those other staff who might have to cover you, and very lastly, support for yourself.

Practical support for DSLs can assist. Computer systems failing, or records not in good order, seem insurmountable, and having the time to change this is added to the 'all too difficult' pile. On top of casework, the DSL may be part of multi-agency meetings, core groups and any manner of safeguarding reviews. They must link in with those responsible for attendance, first aid, health and safety and IT filters to ensure patterns are picked up and children are safe. Many staff approach the DSL in the school corridor to seek advice or pass on concerns which adds to a feeling of pressure. Assistance for your DSLs to put in place robust systems lifts their wellbeing and allows time to reflect on broader, more strategic issues to safeguard children.

Over to you

As part of good quality safeguarding, we need a plan of action to include wellbeing as an integral part of protecting pupils and staff. Useful questions or considerations for your plan might be:

- How can we assist with recognising mental health changes as a possible indicator of abuse in children, and increase the wellbeing of children who have already been identified as being abused?

(Continued)

- How might we ensure the mental wellbeing of all staff is at a level where there is enough reserve to recognise changes to behaviour in children and/or parents and to take action which might not have been planned for?
- How can we better work with parents who may not be recognising safeguarding issues at home due to their own mental health deficit, making it as easy as possible for them to approach us?
- How can we ensure the mental wellbeing of staff who are working in the emotive safeguarding arena, therefore helping to prevent burnout?
- How best might we consider the safeguarding and wellbeing culture within the school and aim to remove toxic positivity in staff interactions and any punitive reaction to behavioural issues in pupils which could be linked to wellbeing?

References

DfE (2020) *Keeping Children Safe in Education*. Available online at: www.gov.uk/government/publications/keeping-children-safe-in-education–2 (Accessed 5 March 2021).

Lukin, K. (2019) 'Toxic Positivity: Don't Always Look on the Bright Side'. *Psychology Today*. Available online at www.psychologytoday.com/gb/blog/the-man-cave/201908/toxic-positivity-dont-always-look-the-bright-side (Accessed 5 March 2021).

Steginus, M. (2019) *Self-Care at Work*. Self-published.

8

GETTING BACK TO GREAT BEHAVIOUR BY BUILDING CONNECTIONS

Mark Goodwin

What?

> Is this job tough? You betcha. Oh God, you betcha. But it is not impossible. We can do this. We're educators. We're born to make a difference.

> (Pierson, 2013: 7:15)

Building connections is fundamental to being a great teacher; connecting young people to your subject, to your school, to learning; above all, helping them to connect to themselves. When there is a human connection in the classroom, behaviour (and therefore wellbeing) mostly takes care of itself. However, connections are hard to build at the best of times; when you have periods of school closure and school absence (as we did during 2020–21) the connection obstacle and the connection challenge is so much more difficult.

Still, teachers and young people have enormous reserves of resilience. They are committed and creative and are far more likely to roll their sleeves up and get on with learning through these vital connections. So, in the spirit of growth mindset, compassion and values-driven, practical and solutions-focused teaching approaches, this chapter will provide some strategies that help to form the sort of connections that get the best behaviour in classrooms (for information on the value of relationships across the whole school, also see Chapter 19, by Sue Roffey). As we know, better classroom behaviour helps to protect and promote teacher wellbeing. Everything we have detailed below is a reminder of values and strategies from teaching wisdom of old, but we all sometimes need reminding of these approaches because they have helped teachers to build connections in the past and are what we need today to really see our young people and help them to connect with learning, school and, ultimately, themselves.

Why?

I have taught young people through the periods of lockdown 2020–21, in mainstream, alternative and special school settings, online and face-to-face, and some things are clear.

The period of disconnection, when students were out of school for weeks and months at a time, exposed some of the weaknesses at the heart of the education system as it stands – maybe this is an opportunity to reframe approaches to behaviour in a different way?

We are human and we all have a range of 'behaviours' to any situation even in a well-connected 'peace time'. If you have all of Maslow's needs dialled in, behaviour responses to learning might be less extreme. But during a period of disconnection, we have seen more extreme responses of behaviour and at a higher frequency, also coming from young people who don't normally display behaviour this way – this may catch even experienced teaching staff out. Our job, as teachers, is to find out where this more frequent unpredictable behaviour is coming from and respond accordingly.

How?

So, what should we be doing to rebuild connections?

First, staff must look after themselves and incorporate into their own wellbeing toolkit the many pieces of excellent advice contained in the other chapters of this book (Chapters 2, 6 and 12 address aspects of self-care for school leaders, for all educators and for early careers teachers respectively); if a teacher's wellbeing is dialled in, it is much easier to act with compassion, empathy and joy in the classroom and start to build the necessary connections with young people.

This chapter provides the means to support teachers' wellbeing by working with young people in a way that encourages good behaviour, because good connections help to generate well-behaved students and a much less stressful environment.

Start rebuilding connection by writing a 'why?' that works for you and the young people you teach. Why are we working on this? Why is it important to work hard now? Why is this important to you? This 'why?' will not generate connection overnight and may be something that has to be revisited over time, but start to write your own story of Covid Recovery and reconnection; try to include the words hope, opportunity, resilience and community. It's almost like a vision board. Young people connect more when they know why they are doing something and what it has to do with them. In the face of disconnection (and for some young people, feelings of hopelessness) help them find their 'why' by first reconnecting them with school. If the school has a powerful recovery narrative, young people will get to hear a narrative counter to more negative scripts in the media and they will have something they can connect their meaning and purpose to. Then, work on your Teacher Why. Teaching is not an easy job, but it is incredibly satisfying because of the meaning and purpose inherent within it. Remind yourself of this and surround yourself with people who share this view.

Work on making your classroom a flexible learning space – throw a wide learning circle – we can do that by role modelling how much we enjoy our lessons, our subject, our school and the company of young people. Most importantly, throw a wide circle on mistakes – have a good script ready for when there is resistance. Be a little more forgiving if a mistake is made or a class rule ignored. Surely it is possible to see school rules as a guide rail and not a straitjacket? This will allow students to stay connected even if they make a mistake.

Restate your sky-high expectations, but accept that the required connections may be slow to achieve. Surround yourself with other staff or senior leaders that understand that the small steps to connection and achievement are massive for some young people – this is especially important when we talk about catch up or deficit. Go for high expectations around the learning process (communication, thought, curiosity) rather than an incessant reminder about their target grade, especially a grade they appear to be miles away from. Much better to keep away from them something they can reject.

Have some empathy and really *see* the young people you teach. Remember this is a shared experience – we have all found recent times difficult and we have all struggled with changes, loss and feelings of disconnection. Every young person has a story, a life outside your classroom, so account for context. Don't cut kids off because of their circumstances. Is the right response to misbehaviour to punish when the roots of that behaviour may lie in extreme difficulties in the home? School is full of data but a young person is a human being, not a set of numbers, so use the data to see the whole glorious and complex picture of the child's life, better understand their context and respond accordingly. Take seeing the young people a step further by taking the time to see what motivates the young people in your class – it might not be your special interest, but showing an interest in their passion will generate positive connections to you and your lesson.

Build in wellbeing check-ins – for yourself and for the young people. Start with the register – not 'yes miss!' but one word about how the student is feeling. This might initially start all too predictably with apathy or jokes but stick with it and kids will more honestly check in. An exam class of 15–16-year-olds started exactly like this, but growing relationships and community led to comments such as 'scared' etc. and the teacher is sending a clear signal that 'I've got to deal with this before I start the lesson….'. This is wellbeing as formative assessment and the teacher has to deal with this before the learning can take place.

Begin with the end of your lesson in mind – look 'up river' from your lesson planning and visualise what you want to see in the classroom. Plan for all the learning that will make your lesson a success, but anticipate the resistance that might appear. Look at your planning with the most disconnected kid in your class in mind. This quick recap of planning is a little onerous but ultimately saves time because you anticipate and can prepare for any resistance and arguments; this will help to ensure all students stay connected to your lesson, and ultimately protects your wellbeing too. If there is resistance or challenge from a student, a script (i.e. something you regularly say if a student says they are bored, confused or not working today) – prepared in advance and regularly used – means you already know what you are going to say if a young person pushes back. A script is common practice in alternative provision schools and helps you to respond and not react: instead of the connection being damaged because of something said in the heat of emotion, the connection is protected because of a measured response.

Over to you

- What action points have you taken from other chapters to support your wellbeing? Plan to work with one action point for the next twenty-one days, starting tomorrow.
- Write a 'Why?' script for your subject and for education/school in general. Use adjectives that inspire, such as potential, empower, opportunity, growth and intelligence.
- Think of a student you can give a fresh start to tomorrow and tell them to begin writing a new story about their education.
- Think of the most disconnected student you teach and look at your lessons through their eyes. What could you change to help them to build a connection?
- What can you do to really see and celebrate the young people you teach? Start by being curious, then ask questions and listen. Young people thrive on the positive interest of a trusted adult, and that must be you.

References

Pierson, R.F. (2013) Every Kid Needs a Champion. TED Talk. Available online at: www.ted.com/talks/rita_pierson_every_kid_needs_a_champion/transcript?language=en (Accessed 5 March 2021).

9

LGBTQ+ PUPILS, STAFF AND WELLBEING

Adele Bates

What?

LGBTQ+ pupils and staff have additional wellbeing and emotional health considerations compared to their non-LGBTQ+ counterparts.

To be clear; being LGBTQ+ does *not* mean that you will have mental health issues; however, it can mean that you are less likely to be accepted in society and more likely to be legally and illegally discriminated against, experience homelessness and suicide. These are some of the situations we know can lead to an increase in mental health issues.

- On the year of the Brexit referendum, LGBTQ+ hate crime went up by 147% in the UK. (Lusher, 2016)

- One in ten people in the UK believe that LGBTQ+ people are 'dangerous' and need to be 'cured'. (Galop, 2019)

- LGBTQ+ people comprise up to 24% of homeless youth in the UK (despite making up 10% of the population in general). (The Big Issue, 2017)

- LGBTQ+ young people are 3.5 times more likely to attempt suicide in the US. (Newport Academy, 2019)

- Almost half of all LGBTQ+ pupils still face bullying at school for being LGBTQ+, and more than two in five trans young people have tried to take their own life. (Stonewall, 2017)

- There are seventy-two countries in the world where LGBTQ+ people face imprisonment. (Human Dignity Trust, n.d.)

- In eleven countries, by law, we could be killed. (Human Dignity Trust, n.d.)

A quick exercise for you and your pupils

- List all of the words you can think of that are offensive towards LGBTQ+ people (and no other characteristic).
- List all of the words you can think of that are offensive towards hetero-sexual, cis-gender people (and no other characteristic).

Which list is longer?

How does that play out in our corridors, in our yards, in our break-times and classrooms?

We know that negative language towards people perceived to be LGBTQ+ is still high in our schools – that is an extra layer of fear, discrimination, negative projection and exclusion that some of our pupils and staff experience on a daily basis. It can be somewhat distracting from your algebra lesson.

This chapter outlines how we can best support our LGBTQ+ pupils and staff within our school communities.

Why?

The negative social context that LGBTQ+ people live has a direct effect upon wellbeing – As an out Bi-teacher, I cannot guarantee I am welcomed or wanted in every school I teach, even in my own country where laws are on my side. At interview, even on application, I and many other LGBTQ+ educators insert small 'tests' to see if a school will be a safe place for us to work, for example, mentioning LGBTQ+ voluntary work on our CV or citing a famous lesbian author in an interview. Schools in many Western countries are not allowed to overtly discriminate, and yet we all know it does, unfortunately, happen.

When LGBTQ+ pupils and staff are welcomed and accepted in schools, they may still face discrimination from outside of school, resulting in having to hold the internal mental and emotional pressure of leading 'double lives.' Despite living in one of the

'Gay Capitals' of Europe, I am still yet to find a school where all of the LGBTQ+ staff feel safe enough to be out to their pupils and school communities. What this lack of safety and belonging does is stop us doing our jobs, and stop our young people learning.

For example, a few years ago, a Year 7 pupil came out to me as gay; they were in the UK temporarily as their parents were on a work visa for two years. They are from a strict Muslim country where being gay is punishable by imprisonment or execution; they wanted to come out to their parents. After acknowledging the pupil's bravery in coming out to me, I asked why they wanted to come out to their parents, and what they thought might be the response – they thought they would be kicked out of the house; we had a safeguarding issue on our hands.

Needless to say, the pupil didn't really grasp the concept of apostrophes in that lesson.

Not feeling safe, battling with prejudice and discrimination, fear and exclusion – for whatever reason – is a barrier to learning, and thus vital for us to address.

Inclusion, belonging, bias awareness and *education* – from all levels throughout our schools – will be the factors that help *all* of our community to feel safe, and thus thrive with education. In some schools this will be a challenge, depending on a school's location, faith practice, resources, community context, etc. However as educators, if we want learning to take place, we have to get safety and belonging right first.

How?

Don't guess.

Question, listen, believe, learn, adapt – rinse and repeat.

Having once seen a documentary about trans people does not mean you will understand the needs of your trans pupil in class 9F3; snogging someone of the same sex in a nightclub once, does not mean you will understand all of the ways in which your LGBTQ+ staff feel excluded by the recruitment process.

Question, listen, believe, learn, adapt – rinse and repeat.

Even better, create systems within your infrastructure that support this process and have regular points of re-evaluation, student and staff voice and up-to-date training.

Firstly, consider what it is that you want to find out. Some ideas: how safe LGBTQ+ pupils feel, whether LGBTQ+ staff feel included, whether pupils find LGBTQ+ role models within their favourite subject, how many of your behaviour issues are related to homo/bi/transphobia, whether staff teaching Personal, Social, Health and Economic Education (PSHE) and Relationships, Sex and Health Education (RSHE) feel confident in being able to answer questions about LGBTQ+ sex or support pupils transitioning their gender, whether staff and pupils regularly hear offensive language towards LGBTQ+ people in your school, whether pupils are bullied for being, or being perceived to be, LGBTQ+, whether your RSHE curriculum covers the now compulsory (in the UK and some other countries for *all* schools) aspect of LGBTQ+ relationships and families, whether prospective same-sex or transgender parents and carers would consider sending their children to your school, whether there is homo/bi/transphobia amongst your staff, whether LGBTQ+ staff feel confident enough to be part of senior leadership.

Once you've chosen the topic, choose the best way to find the answers – remembering that some people will want to answer anonymously, some are better at discussing face-to-face, some will like tick boxes. Check your data, your lesson resources, your staff recruitment process and outcomes, your library shelves.

It can be useful to get an outside perspective or specialist to help with this process and help remove yours and your school's *own* bias. I once worked with a school who had an out LGBTQ+ headteacher. Due to their own challenges of being out as a teacher through the years, they often approached LGBTQ+ education more cautiously than some of the hetero-cis headteachers I have worked with – we *all* have our blind spots.

Once you identify your areas for improvement, get a range of pupils and staff on board to create active solutions and interventions. Some ideas:

- LGBTQ+ awareness training for *all* staff (including cleaners, support staff, admin staff) – ensure you cover curriculum, mental health, disclosures, safeguarding, sex, health, law and relationships.

- Create LGBTQ+ safe spaces (these could be physical spaces or times – note, these are not for LGBTQ+ people only, but for anyone to discuss these topics safely. I have seen pupils come to these and ask how they can better support their LGBTQ+ friends or family).

- Create LGBTQ+ or Equalities allies.

- Education evenings for parents and carers – remember, LGBTQ+ issues are addressed very differently in many Western countries now than they were 15, 20, 30 years ago. They may have genuine questions about the values and education their children are receiving.

- Provide LGBTQ+ counselling.

Remember, just because a member of staff or pupil identifies as LGBTQ+, that does not mean that they necessarily want to get involved in public activities. We all have a right to decide how much of ourselves we feel safe in bringing out, no one should be forced to; there may be a very real safety reason why they can't.

Equally, don't assume everyone knows how to teach or support this topic. In the same way as you wouldn't expect all staff to know how to teach volcanoes, staff will need training in order to support LGBTQ+ wellbeing, and possibly sensitive and safeguarding-related disclosures, positively.

A note on the law, objections, parents and carers

Talking about LGBTQ+ awareness, education and health can, for some people, be a challenging topic. In my experience, it is very rarely the pupils who have the issue in the West – they have been brought up in a progressively accepting society. It is more likely to be staff or parents and carers who have concerns.

The key here is communication. Unfortunately, some people can assume that supporting LGBTQ+ wellbeing means talking about sex or 'converting' people, so when there are objections or fears, find out what those fears are exactly first; you may be able to reassure around a lot of them quite easily. In the Relationships and Sex and Health Education (RSHE) Curriculum in England, compulsory from September 2020 (find out more about how careful implementation of this curriculum supports wellbeing, in Chapter 23 by John Rees), all pupils are to be taught about LGBTQ+ families and relationships. A media headline might scream '4-year-olds learn about anal sex!'; this is not the case. The curriculum has been developed to age appropriately introduce all sorts of different families and relationships – so the 4-year-olds might learn that some people live with Gran, some with Dad and Daddy and some with Mum and Dad – they would not learn about any forms of sex. Whilst 11–14-year-old pupils may learn that anal sex is an act that any gender may partake in, including heterosexual couples – and the importance of consent and health around any sexual interactions.

The Equality Act 2010 now prevents schools from discriminating against who they support or teach – so if your trans pupils are not receiving teaching around relationships and sex in a way that will keep them healthy and safe, there is an issue. Schools, as public bodies, have a duty to uphold the law, and you may need to bring specialists in.

The inspection body Ofsted (the Office for Standards in Education, Children's Services and Skills in England) now also stands behind this. As part of their inspections they can 'deep dive' into RSHE content in the same way as any other compulsory curriculum component. They also look at a school's evidence of homo/bi/transphobic bullying and what is being done to address the issue, re-educate and support.

When working with staff who have been teaching a long time, I find these simple facts about duty of care can help reassure fears. Some staff may have been teaching during a time in which even mentioning LGBTQ+ people could have lost them their job – and many had to hide themselves just to work in a school. A lot has changed quickly; it helps to show people that there is safety, support *and* the law now on the side of putting *all* staff and pupils' wellbeing first.

A word on being wrong

When discussing people's identities, things can be sensitive and ever-changing – the language, the laws and what's possible. The foundation to this work is strong, safe communication – spaces where people can ask, sometimes feel icky, uncomfortable, but feel supported enough to learn – and we always are; if you are reading this and feel there's something I have missed here, please let me know – because the more we listen, learn and adapt, the more we can create safe, healthy and engaging learning environments for our whole school communities.

Over to you

The following questions are posed to help school communities effectively support the additional wellbeing and emotional health considerations for LGBTQ+ pupils and staff:

- What do you want to achieve? Write down a few sentences to summarise your overall vision for supporting LGBTQ+ wellbeing in your classroom or school.
- What steps do you need to take to achieve your vision? What are the timescales for these steps?
- Who else do you need to involve?

References

Equality Act (2010). c. 15. Available online at: www.legislation.gov.uk/ukpga/2010/15/contents (Accessed 28 March 2021).

Galop (2019). Press Release: Hate Crime Report 2019. Available online at: www.galop.org.uk/press-release-hate-crime-report-2019/ (Accessed 6 January 2021).

Human Dignity Trust (n.d.). Map of Countries that Criminalise LGBT People. Available online at: www.humandignitytrust.org/lgbt-the-law/map-of-criminalisation/ (Accessed 3 March 2021).

Lusher, A. (2016). Homophobic attacks rose 147 per cent after the Brexit vote. *The Independent.* Available online at: www.independent.co.uk/news/uk/home-news/brexit-hate-crime-hatred-homophobia-lgbt-147-cent-rise-double-attacks-gays-lesbians-transsexuals-post-referendum-racism-eu-referendum-xenophobia-racists-farage-ukip-a7352411.html (Accessed 6 January 2021).

Newport Academy (2019). LGBT+ Suicide Statistics Show Greater Risk Among Young Teens. Available at: www.newportacademy.com/resources/mental-health/lgbt-suicide-statistics/ (Accessed 6 January 2021).

Stonewall (2017). School Report (2017). Available online at: www.stonewall.org.uk/resources/school-report-2017 (Accessed 3 March 2021).

The Big Issue (2017). Why are so many young LGBT people in Britain homeless? Available online at: www.bigissue.com/latest/many-young-lgbt-people-britain-homeless/ (Accessed 6 January 2021).

10

THE WATER IS DRAINING AWAY — BURNOUT AND RETENTION

Stephen Waters

What?

This chapter highlights the wellbeing and mental health crisis in our schools. It describes Freudenberger's (1974) twelve stages of burnout and presents the *Waters Index of Teacher Burnout*, which enables staff to assess their level of risk. This is followed by a detailed look at Maslach's (2008) six factors of burnout and how to prevent and tackle burnout at a whole school level.

Why?

... the penultimate day before the Easter break, I eventually broke down in front of a class. The poor handful of students that wanted to learn in this class – their enthusiasm for learning had slowly declined; their patience for others dwindled. I hated seeing this and burst into tears in front of the whole class, and between sobs I ranted about how much I wanted them to achieve and do well, but that chosen behaviours were holding them and their peers back. By the end of the lesson, I felt embarrassed and ashamed for my emotional outburst.

I tried to enjoy the Easter break but instead I ended up working most of it, marking assessments and planning for the next term. When I returned to school, I couldn't do it.

I walked into my classroom and walked right back out again. The anxiety was too much. I walked away. I made my way inside the main building; a member of staff caught me, asked if I was okay. That was it, their concern set me off and tears just streamed. I sat in the meeting room for what felt like hours, just sobbing. I eventually went home, not that I remember how I got there. The rest of the day is a complete blur.

I couldn't return the next day or the next and eventually I was signed off.

Hewett (2019: xxvii–xxviii)

This sad and moving account, from Victoria Hewett, Head of Humanities and author of *Making it as a Teacher: How to Survive and Thrive in the First Five Years* (Hewett, 2019), is typical of teachers suffering from burnout. The body and mind shut down, overwhelmed by attempts to cope with high levels of physical and mental exhaustion that have built up over a long period of time.

Fortunately, Victoria – active on Twitter as @MrsHumanities – applied to a different school and, with the right support, was able to rekindle her love of teaching and continue to develop her successful career. She is now an advocate for 'Education Support', the charity for teachers which has a 24-hour helpline and which supported Victoria through her mental breakdown.

What is burnout?

Some teachers become so worn down by relentless accountability, excessive workload and the stress of the job, that they end up leaving a profession they originally entered with optimism, excitement and promise. We are in a retention crisis that can only be solved by focusing on the wellbeing and mental health of our teachers. Experienced teachers and recently qualified teachers alike are leaving the profession. According to a House of Commons Briefing Paper (Foster, 2019), around 42,000 teachers hand in their notice each year. Almost a third of teachers resign within five years of qualifying. The *Guardian* newspaper (Weale, 2019) reported data from the National Education Union (NEU) that showed that one in five teachers (18%) planned to leave the profession within two years, while 'two-fifths of teachers, school leaders and support staff want to quit in the next five years – blaming "out of control" workload pressures and "excessive" accountability…' (Weale, 2019: paragraph 1). Tempting more recruits won't stop teachers leaving. We can keep filling the bath, but the water's draining away.

We need effective whole school approaches (see Chapter 1, by Frederika Roberts). Teachers can adopt self-care strategies to reduce their own mental ill-health, but if their schools do not take responsibility for the stress caused by the organisation itself, there will be continual and relentless individual battles that some teachers will inevitably lose.

According to Michel (2016: paragraph 13), burnout occurs, 'when the balance of deadlines, working hours and other stressors outstrips rewards, recognition and relaxation'.

In *Scientific American*, Kraft (2006), a German science writer, describes how psychologists Herbert Freudenberger and Gail North identified twelve phases of burnout, culminating in total breakdown, where the sufferer requires medical intervention.

The twelve stages (Freudenberger, 1974, as cited in Kraft, 2006) are:

1. A compulsion to prove oneself

2. Working harder

3. Neglecting self-care

4. Displacement of conflicts (where the source of burnout is attributed to events which did not cause it)

5. Re-consideration of personal values as isolation, conflict avoidance and denial of physical needs occurs

6. Denial of problems

7. Withdrawal

8. Negative behavioural changes, e.g., lack of confidence and apathy

9. Depersonalisation

10. Inner emptiness

11. Clinical depression

12. Mental and physical collapse, with suicidal thoughts/actions.

I have customised the stages to provide teachers with a scale to assess their level of burnout in the Waters Index of Teacher Burnout (V3) (see Figure 10.1).

Christina Maslach of the University of Berkeley in California has been researching burnout since the 1970s and is a recognised world expert. Maslach co-authored the *Maslach Burnout Inventory (MBI)* (Maslach et al., 1986) with Susan E. Jackson; it aims to assess an individual's risk of succumbing to three components that combine to form burnout (Maslach, 2008):

•   Emotional exhaustion – characterised by irritability, permanent tiredness, nausea, stomach pains and an inability to focus.

•   Lack of personal accomplishment – self-blame, lack of confidence, feeling a failure, not doing a good job.

(Based on Freudenberger's 12 Stages)
Tick statement that best describes your behaviour and emotions

Stage	My behaviour and emotions
1	I must prove myself and show my headteacher and leaders that I am a good teacher and can do what I was appointed to do. I like giving myself challenges and achieving them. Perhaps I should aim higher.
2	I must set myself high standards and can't afford to say 'No' in case people think I'm not committed. I find it difficult to take time off and to have a good work-life balance. I want to get ahead of deadlines and find it difficult to prioritise tasks.
3	I am not looking after myself properly, but preparation and marking must come first. I know I shouldn't work as late as I do. I wish I could have more time off at weekends. I am making mistakes I didn't use to make.
4	I feel resentful of my friends who leave work behind when they go home. I feel a bit empty and I am often exhausted. I've noticed I'm getting headaches and aches and pains and sometimes feel sick. I'm worried about school. I am forgetting to do things.
5	I feel as if I'm on autopilot and emotionally spaced-out. My whole life is taken up by work. I'm neglecting family and friends.
6	I prefer to be on my own. I often feel angry and I lose my temper with pupils and sometimes staff. I know it's due to workload and setting myself high standards. I've had a few days off recently.
7	I feel isolated and retreat to my classroom. That one drink I have to relax in the evening has increased to two or three. I sometimes self-medicate to get through the day. I have a hangover sometimes which makes teaching so hard in the morning.
8	I've changed so much since I first qualified. I used to be outgoing, but I think staff are avoiding me. I've had to go to see my GP and she has put me on anti-depressants. I look stressed and drawn and worn out.
9	What's the point of teaching if it is destroying me? I keep going but I don't enjoy it like I used to. The medication is helping but I feel tired all day. I can't think beyond the next lesson. I find it difficult to plan and to look ahead.
10	I feel empty and lost. I am eating too much to comfort myself. I feel that there is no one to help me.
11	I am so depressed. I am lonely. I can't see any light at the end of the tunnel. Even when I sleep, I get up exhausted. I feel so guilty that I'm doing such a bad job and letting the children down. I don't enjoy anything. I don't know how much longer I can take it. Perhaps I'd be better off out of it.
12	I can't face going in. I can hardly get out of bed. I'm losing weight. I feel anxious and guilty. I can't face it any more. I am wondering if I have the courage to put an end to my life.

Figure 10.1   The Waters Index of Teacher Burnout V3 (Waters, 2021)

Stages 1-3: Opportunity to reduce impact via self-help or accepting help from others. 4-6: Need to seek professional help, such as counselling, to prevent further decline of health. 7-9: Urgent professional help a necessity. 10-12: Emergency help needed, especially at Stage 12 where there is a threat to life.

- Depersonalisation – cynicism, isolation, distancing from work and colleagues, blame and negativity directed towards others. As teachers spend most of their working time with pupils, negativity can be directed towards pupils, especially if behaviour is poor, creating a cycle where pupils themselves react with negativity and cause teachers further stress.

How?

How to tackle burnout

Workload is often identified as the cause of burnout. It is undoubtedly the case that workload in the education profession is excessive and has a considerable and negative impact on teachers' work-life balance and family life. Since the 2019 update to the Ofsted (the Office for Standards in Education, Children's Services and Skills in England) inspection framework (Ofsted, 2019), consideration of teachers' workload now forms part of a school's Leadership and Management judgement.

While it is crucial that schools reduce teachers' workload, Maslach (2008) observes that, whilst it is generally perceived that work-related stress is one-dimensional and based on excessive workload, hers and Jackson's burnout model (Maslach et al., 1986) refers to six workplace discrepancies.

Ofsted's wellbeing support level expectations can be achieved by addressing these discrepancies. So, what are the six factors, and how can we relate them to an educational context? In no particular order, they are:

1) Work overload

When the quantity of work required exceeds the time available, or when a job is simply too difficult for an employee's current resources.

2) Lack of control

There is a lack of professional trust; decision-making is reduced to following instructions; judgements on teaching and learning quality are made by line managers and leaders; teachers have restricted access to resources; curriculum design is decided by others; data collection is mandated and scrutinised; and teachers' effectiveness is judged on their results.

3) Lack of reward

Not necessarily just pay – social recognition, acknowledgement of effort, praise and thanks are just as important, if not more so.

4) Absence of community

In her book, Maslach (2008) states that when people compliment and comfort, as well as share humour and joy with, people they care about and respect, they will be at their best and flourish in a sense of community.

5) Lack of fairness

A commonly held perception that promotions are biased, that there is favouritism and/ or the sense that some staff are more appreciated, and thus more frequently rewarded, than others.

6) Conflict of values

When a teacher's values – the reason they entered teaching in the first place – clash with the educational values of the Department for Education (DfE) and government. If a school endorses the government's emphasis on 'standards' by placing overriding importance on academic results rather than valuing mental health and relationships, the conflict can erode a teacher's identity and their sense of moral purpose.

Preventing burnout

Under the Health and Safety at Work Act (1974), an employer has a duty of care for their employees. While reducing mental ill-health is as important as taking care of employees' physical health, it is the latter which receives most attention, with a focus on reducing the risk of accidents in the workplace. In order to reduce burnout, schools need to mitigate the adverse impacts of government policies, strategies and directives. Schools that have a very strong culture of staff wellbeing and mental health protect their staff by refusing to engage in high-stakes accountability (See Waters, 2021: Chapter 6). By addressing Maslach's six factors, your school can achieve this.

Step 1

The first step is to rank the six factors in the order in which they are having an adverse impact on staff wellbeing, placing the factor which has the most negative impact in first place. You can do this by surveying staff individually and anonymously or by organising a card sort activity during a scheduled meeting, where the six factors can be provided on sets of cards for pairs or groups to place in rank order.

Step 2

The next step is to ask staff why each of those factors are causing burnout and note the responses.

Possible causes of burnout

Examples of causes of burnout: Excessive marking requirements; ineffective behaviour policies; inconsistent leadership; failure to take teachers' views into account; lack of thanks or acknowledgement for the work staff are doing; division and competition between teachers in different year groups and/or departments, identifying poor 'performers'; poor internal communication; feedback characterised by aggression and lack of respect; and bullying and harassment.

Step 3

Draw up an action plan for how you intend to tackle these causes and circulate it to staff for anonymous comment. Make adjustments and begin to implement it. Monitor impact as you go, using short, anonymised online surveys.

Figure 10.2 shows a simple action plan grid.

Maslach factor	Position in rank order /6. Greatest adverse impact first.	Negative impact	What action will you take?	Who else will be involved?	When will you take action?

Figure 10.2   Action Plan - Tackling and Preventing Burnout

Step 4

Once this work has concluded, evaluate its impact and ask your staff to rank Maslach's six factors again. If there has been progress, factors that previously had the greatest impact should have moved down the ranking.

Step 5

Finally, plan further actions for the following twelve months, as part of a three-year rolling programme, and make the process a permanent addition to your School Development Plan.

Over to you

The process of tackling burnout is challenging and requires time, if it is to be prevented in future – at least one academic year for the roll-out of your initial action plan. It also requires openness, transparency and a willingness on the part of leadership to accept criticism and acknowledge the need for whole school change.

In turn, there needs to be a recognition that stress affects everyone – including the headteacher and all non-teaching support staff (see Chapter 21 by Kimberley Evans) – and it is important to resist apportioning blame. The end goal is to create a supportive staff community which enables everyone to ask anyone else for help and support. And that includes senior members of staff being able to ask, for example, an NQT for advice.

Creating such a community entails whole school change to implement a culture of staff wellbeing and mental health, moving from an environment in which staff are fighting lonely battles against burnout, to one where every adult in the school benefits from mutual support. Placing responsibility on staff for their self-care in an uncaring or toxic school environment is like telling someone who is homeless to find somewhere to live, while maintaining the conditions in which they became homeless in the first place. School leadership and governing bodies/boards have a duty of care for their staff and this entails systemic implementation. It is only by schools taking responsibility for staff physical and mental health that self-care will be effective – it is a balance between the two. If your school commits to this cultural change, you will not only banish burnout, but you will also create a caring school, where teachers are happy to stay, rather than counting down the days until they can leave.

Use the reflection points below to consider what steps you can take to eliminate burnout in your school.

- Rank the burnout factors for yourself.
- Consider why each of those might put you at risk of burnout personally.
- Draw up an action plan for tackling these to reduce your personal risk of burnout.
- Follow steps 1 to 5 outlined in this chapter with your staff.

References

Foster, D. (2019) Teacher recruitment and Retention in England (House of Commons Library briefing paper 7222). Available online at: https://researchbriefings.files.parliament.uk/documents/CBP-7222/CBP-7222.pdf (Accessed 27 March 2021).

Freudenberger, H.J. (1974) 'Staff burnout.' *Journal of Social Issues*, 30: 159–65.

Health and Safety at Work Act 1974, c. 37. Available online at: www.legislation.gov.uk/ukpga/1974/37/contents (Accessed 27 March 2021).

Hewett, V. (2019) *Making it as a Teacher: How to Survive and Thrive in the First Five Years.* Abingdon and New York, NY: Routledge.

Kraft, U. (2006) 'Burned Out.' *Scientific American*, 17(3): 28–33.

Maslach, C., Jackson, S.E., Leiter, M.P., Schaufeli, W.B. and Schwab, R.L. (1986) 'Maslach burnout inventory' 21: 3463–64. Palo Alto, CA: Consulting Psychologists Press.

Maslach, C. (2008) *Banishing Burnout.* San Francisco: Jossey-Bass.

Michel, A. (2016) Burnout and the Brain. *Association for Psychological Science.* Available online at: www.psychologicalscience.org/observer/burnout-and-the-brain (Accessed 2 March 2021).

Ofsted (2019) School inspection handbook (EIF). Available online at: www.gov.uk/government/publications/school-inspection-handbook-eif (Accessed 2 March 2021).

Waters, S. (2021) 'Teacher Burnout, Ofsted, Wellbeing and Mental Health' in Stephen Waters (ed.), *Cultures of Wellbeing and Mental Health in Schools.* Maidenhead: Open University Press McGraw-Hill.

Weale, S. (2019) Fifth of teachers plan to leave profession within two years. *The Guardian.* Available online at: www.theguardian.com/education/2019/apr/16/fifth-of-teachers-plan-to-leave-profession-within-two-years (Accessed 2 March 2021).

11

HOW DO WE ADDRESS WELLBEING IN A CULTURE OF ASSESSMENT?

Alison Kriel

What?

The aim of this chapter is to consider how we navigate our way through a culture of assessment and ensure the wellbeing of our pupils. I share some of the practices we developed in my school, which supported the wellbeing of my pupils and enhanced their success in national assessments.

Teaching is the best job in the world. It's fun, rewarding, fulfilling, and every day is different. I've yet to meet a teacher, especially one who teaches from the soul, who made the life changing decision to become a teacher to enable children to pass exams, and most tell me that what they love most about teaching is that it gives you the opportunity to have a real impact on the lives of others. Teachers know they are force multipliers and their impact spreads through every student they reach.

In the UK, most children spend fifteen years in school – almost all of their childhood. It is a travesty that, for many, what defines whether those years were successful or not is a set of numbers in a box when they leave. We need to see our pupils as more than data, more than numbers in a box. The truth is that, for most pupils, the majority of what we assess is forgotten and they learn it simply to pass exams. Those grades can open a door to a first job or to a place at university, but that is becoming less important as employers realise that straight-A students do not necessarily make the best employees. At a meeting I recently attended with some of the biggest corporations in the world, they told us that grades are less important than employees who are collaborative, creative thinkers, self-disciplined, reflective, resilient, adaptable, able to accept difference and work as part of a diverse team, share ideas, willing to take risks, and can manage change. We mislead our pupils and their parents when we allow them to believe that grades and assessments are the gateway to opportunity. That may have been the case decades ago, but it is no longer the case.

Why?

Assessment is an integral part of our education system, but going into it with a positive mindset and a toolbox of strategies for being well is the key to success.

When I was a headteacher, I knew we had to ensure that our pupils did well in their assessments, but I was determined that this was not our core purpose. I wanted them to have the best opportunities to be the best global citizens, to be confident in knowing they had the skills they needed to be self-sustaining and successful. I wanted our pupils to be happy, independent, confident, proud of who they are – to have positive self-esteem and self-belief. I wanted them to know that they were successful. For many of us, the clever kids are the ones who are good at English, maths and science. I wanted the pupils in my school to know that everyone is clever.

I did not want to find out who the best leaders, innovators, creatives, problem solvers, collaborators, musicians, and artists were only once they had completed their Standard Attainment Tests (SATs) and we allowed all those unique skills to emerge in their leavers' show or during the final residential trip. For me, that felt like a missed opportunity to know our pupils well and to be part of their success. We therefore made it our responsibility to know each child's strengths on entry to the school, and placed equal value on parent and child information as we did on teacher evaluation. Once identified, we then worked hard to provide each child with as many opportunities as possible to reach greater depth in their areas of strength. Every child was celebrated and had an opportunity to shine. And value was placed on every area of the curriculum, including the unmeasured curriculum.

As a staff, we understood that self-esteem impacts everything we do, how we interact with each other, and develop resilience. It also impacts directly on academic performance. Low self-esteem leads to an unwillingness to take risks, a fear of making mistakes, to limited ambition. We knew that there was a correlation between exam success and positive self-esteem and put that at the heart of our work. Purposeful actions included regularly showing each child how far they had come. Workbooks were beautiful and valued, and the children knew to look at their work from the start of the year to where they were to see progress. We actively looked for opportunities for praise and celebration.

This included pupils celebrating each other and knowing what everyone's gold was – their special interest and what they did best. Parents were invited in three times a year for one-to-one conferences and the discussions were often led by the children showing what they were most proud of. We wanted our parents and pupils to move beyond asking what the children needed to know to do well in their SATs to valuing the whole curriculum. We came to realise that the better the children felt about themselves as learners, the less they feared getting things wrong, the more willing they were to take risks in their learning. We actively set out to break away from a system in which our children develop a fear of getting things wrong because we know from personal experience that we learn most from the times when things do not go to plan.

How?

We developed a school culture where every child felt valued, celebrated and a part of the community, and delivered a curriculum in which they could see themselves reflected. Belonging is integral to positive self-esteem.

Early identification of need is as important as early recognition of success. Delayed assessment leads to poor self-esteem, overwhelm and negativity. Delayed assessment also leads to more expensive, time-consuming interventions, so investing in early assessment and support is essential. We prioritised investment in solid foundations to increase equity of opportunity rather than playing catch-up once failure, fear, low self-esteem and low morale is established. Teaching and learning from a place of adversity is not joyful. We believed that every child had a right to an enriched curriculum. There is nothing worse than having to do additional lessons in something you hate while the rest of your peers get to do something you do well and you love. It denies an opportunity for success and for you to be celebrated.

When it was time for SATs, the children went in knowing the likely outcomes before they went in. They knew they were successful. They knew they were well-taught. They trusted their teachers and their teachers trusted them to do their best. For a small minority, there was a barrier to reaching age expectation – if they were on the ASD spectrum, for example. We simply asked every child to do their best, which is the most we can hope for in anyone. Staff, pupils and parents knew that tests were important but they also knew that a disappointing result was a fraction of life and did not define failure any more than obtaining the best grades in exams at age 18 ensured success and happiness. We talked about career paths for academic success but also invited in creatives, entrepreneurs and explorers who live incredible lives despite a few falls along the way. We spent time helping the children to understand what happiness and fulfilment looks like rather than hedonistic pleasure and playing it safe through a narrow definition of success.

All our pupils learned about wellbeing, and the need to be responsible for themselves. They had a toolbox of strategies for self-regulation of their behaviour. Everyone accessed an outdoor curriculum through Forest School and physical education. They knew that poor sleep, lack of exercise and too much screen time affected their mood. Our catering team took pride in preparing delicious, healthy vegetarian meals (which avoided having to decide whether to serve halal or haram meat and kept costs down considerably). Dessert was fruit only and we were a water only school. Take up was high amongst pupils and staff. Food in school rules applied to the very small number of pupils who had packed lunches, and we were proud that parents co-operated with the request. A mindfulness teacher came in termly to support whole school practice and every class had three mindfulness sessions daily. Our wellbeing curriculum served the children well when doing their SATs. No homework was set as it was important that everyone felt rested and had leisure time. We asked that everyone went to bed at a reasonable time and avoided sugar. And amazingly, everyone did. Each morning started with a dance session, followed by a meditation. During the test they had a piece of fruit if they needed a sugar hit and a bottle of water for the moments they needed a bit of a think. The children had a positive mindset, knew they belonged, knew they were celebrated and accepted for who they were. They were happy and healthy and behaviour was excellent. We all knew and cherished that we were part of a highly successful community.

That was not always the case. There was a time when the school was a failing community. Pupil attainment was very low, pupil behaviour was unacceptable, the curriculum was very narrow and SATs-focussed. There was an over-emphasis on interventions and catch up, which only led to boredom and disappointment. Teachers were not trusted, morale was low, staff retention was low. Pupils were discussed as statistical units and staff were over-observed and numbered based on Ofsted – the Office for Standards in Education, Children's Services and Skills in England – criteria. Schools are about human connection (see also Chapters 8 and 19) and a failure to see that turns our schools into exam factories and pupils into products. That is the ultimate tragedy and denies a joy in teaching and learning. Finding joy was the key to our success.

Amazing things happen when you tell your staff that they are doing well and you develop a culture of openness and transparency. Amazing things happen when, together, you learn that less is more, that we can be more productive by reducing our working hours. Amazing things happen when you reduce the time spent teaching a narrow curriculum to enable more pupils to feel like successful learners. Amazing things happen when time is invested in the unmeasured curriculum. Amazing things happen when there is a whole school approach to wellbeing where each individual is encouraged to value their time, their thoughts, their actions, their strengths. Amazing things happen when everyone knows that they belong and that they are valued members of the community. Amazing things happen when there's a culture of celebration.

Over to you

As we consider wellbeing in a culture of assessment, we need a plan of action to consider a better way forward.

- What are the key things that schools need to ensure for all of our pupils that enable positive self-esteem, which is integral to their wellbeing?

(Continued)

- What would you put into a toolbox of wellbeing strategies for your pupils to use so that they can cope well with the demands placed on them in light of assessments?
- Assessment is a part of school life that is valued by many and is not going to disappear. Is there a way for us to do it differently so that it supports pupil and teacher wellbeing?

12

THE ROLE OF SELF-CARE IN RETAINING EARLY CAREER TEACHERS

Stephen Waters

What?

In Chapter 3, the importance of underpinning support strategies for Early Career Teachers (ECTs) with a commitment to whole school staff wellbeing and mental health was emphasised. The role of employers and organisations in providing a 'well' environment and workplace culture is increasingly being recognised, not only as vital to employees' wellbeing, but also as a legal obligation within the employer's duty of care. There is a balance to be struck between the school looking after us and the care we take of ourselves.

In this chapter, we will explore the role and importance of self-care in retaining ECTs. We identify six components of self-care. We suggest how you can take better care of yourself by focusing on each component and taking positive action. This will tackle aspects of your life where you are not taking sufficient care of yourself and prevent your health being further put at risk in the future.

Why?

The importance of self-care in teaching

Victoria Hewett, in her wonderfully practical book for ECTs, *Making it as a Teacher* draws our attention to how we have individual tolerances and responses to the challenging work of teaching:

...we need to understand the impact our work has on our physical and mental health. Each of us can tolerate different levels of stress. We each approach our wellbeing differently, and we all have variations to what it means to have a work-life balance.

(Hewett, 2019: 151)

Bucky Yusuf makes a similar point in her chapter in the Chartered College's *Early Career Framework Handbook* (Yusuf, 2020). She also refers helpfully to Lexico's definitions of 'wellbeing' and 'work-life balance':

Wellbeing - the state of being comfortable, healthy or happy.

(Lexico, 2019a)

Work-life balance - the division of one's time and focus between working and family or leisure activities.

(Lexico, 2019b)

Hewett reminds us that '... teaching is a job, not a lifestyle' (2019: 151) and suggests to teachers who are struggling that they carry out an audit of what they like and dislike about teaching, identifying factors that are within and outside their control. Focusing on what is within your control and learning to cope with factors outside it prevents energy being spent on what you are unable to change.

Similarly, Hewett refers to Alex Quigley's blog 'The Confident Teacher' (Quigley, n.d.) which defines two types of time. There is time that is allocated to us which we are unable to change, e.g., our teaching timetable. On the other hand, there is time within our control and which we allocate ourselves, e.g., planning lessons or going for a walk. In this time, we are in control of self-care. How we allocate this time has a significant impact on how we cope with time we are unable to change.

One of the most important teacher truths is that you will never finish your work – ever. Teachers tend to be self-motivators and to set themselves high standards. They are conscientious and want to finish their work. Many teachers are, in Belbin's definition of the roles of team members, 'completer-finishers' (Belbin, n.d.) and derive satisfaction from seeing their 'to do' list all ticked off. This won't work in teaching. There is always something left to do. Do what you don't want to do first, especially if it is a priority. Constantly having that task that you are dreading at the back of your mind increases your anxiety and reduces your ability to concentrate on the task you are tackling now.

Set a time limit on tasks. Include family and friends time in your plans and get used to walking away from tasks that can wait or that can be done in half the time if you are prepared not to seek perfection.

How?

The components of self-care

According to Butler et al. (2019: 107–24), there are six domains of self-care:

- Physical
- Psychological
- Emotional
- Spiritual
- Relational
- Professional.

Using these categories, how can you improve your self-care and reduce the impact of teaching on your physical and mental health?

Firstly, rank them in the order in which poor self-care is having an adverse impact on your physical and/or mental health. For example, if a lack of social life is affecting your mental health more than the other categories, rank it as the category to tackle first. Then, consider using the following strategies below to address each category, with the aim of reducing its negative impact. The categories are presented as above, although, of course, your rank order may be different.

If you have any concerns about your physical or mental health, you should seek medical advice. Although the self-care tips below broadly follow those provided on public health sites, such as the National Health Service (NHS) in the UK, our proposed strategies might not be appropriate in your case, especially if you have a medical condition. If in doubt, seek advice from your doctor.

Physical self-care

Eat regularly, little and often, rather than infrequently having large meals. Make time for breakfast, even if it means setting the alarm earlier. Try to eat healthily, at least once a day. Drink water/other fluids throughout the day, including during lessons. Dehydration can lead to a number of negative physical responses: feeling hungry, headaches, lack of concentration, low energy, irritability, stomach pains. Consider taking multi-vitamin supplements, especially during winter, and get sufficient sleep (not easy, if you have young children). Try to get into a routine where you relax for twenty to thirty minutes, without TV or phone, before preparing for bed. Some teachers find practising mindfulness is beneficial in both reducing stress and calming them, ready for sleep. If getting a good night's sleep is impossible, a twenty-minute nap after work will help your body and mind to rest.

Aim to exercise each day. It doesn't have to be aerobic to be beneficial. Even a daily walk of ten minutes will improve your physical health. While teaching, you will already be taking a surprising number of daily steps. A walk outside, especially during summertime when you can pay attention to your surroundings, is, of course, a more beneficial kind of exercise, as you can also rest your mind as you walk.

Psychological self-care

Practise mindfulness. There are a number of mindfulness courses online – some of them free or low cost – and a number of free apps that you can download to your phone. Here is an exercise you can practise:

1. Sitting or standing, place both feet flat on the ground. Place your feet hip-width apart.

2. Breathe in for a count of four.

3. Hold your breath for a count of four.

4. Release your breath for a count of four.

5. Let your breath in flow deep down into your abdomen, without forcing it.

6. Breathe in through your nose and out through your mouth.

7. Repeat. Even two-three cycles of breathing in and breathing out have a calming effect.

Write a diary or daily journal to record what has gone well during your teaching day. Document your challenges, how you dealt with them and, if appropriate, how you might have approached them differently. Practise self-compassion: be kind to yourself. This often involves challenging your self-critical internal dialogue or perfectionism.

Jamie Thom in his book *Teacher Resilience* (Thom, 2020) quotes Dr Kristin Neff, creator of the Self-compassion Scales:

> With the burnout issues teachers face, taking care of themselves through work-life balance is important, but isn't enough. Teachers need to give themselves permission to be self-compassionate for the stress they're under.
>
> (Neff, as cited in Thom, 2020: 41)

Tell yourself that, given the challenges you are facing – either in your work or home life, or both – you are 'good enough'. For example, if a lesson has not gone well, you might say to yourself, 'That was dreadful. I'm just no good at teaching eleven-year-olds. I don't know if I can continue teaching. Other teachers seem to cope. Why can't I?' A self-compassionate internal dialogue would run something like this: 'That lesson didn't go well. However, it wasn't all bad. Some things went well, such as the silent writing task. I am not sleeping well, and this is affecting my energy and patience. I am also worried about my baby who is ill. I did my best and this is good enough right now. I know I could do better if I was sleeping properly and not anxious about my baby'.

Emotional self-care

Suppressed negative emotions often lead to adverse physical reactions: for example, headaches or stomach disorders, as well as psychological effects, such as anxiety and depression. It is important to share your emotional responses to the issues you face at work. If there is no one at school that you can talk to, share with your partner, friend or family. Some couples have found it helpful to have a time-limited kind of debrief where they talk about their day for, say, ten or fifteen minutes at a pre-arranged time. Although this sounds formal, it ensures that time is set aside for each partner to share their emotions and feelings. If it is not possible to offload to someone at home, journaling can be used to record how your day has gone. Some teachers find that they can create a dialogue with themselves through their journal, which helps them to be self-reflective.

Spiritual self-care

Spiritual self-care does not have to be religious, although some teachers find belief through religion is a source of support. Try to connect with nature by taking a walk. Deliberately notice sounds and sights around you, rather than becoming immersed in thoughts about work. Mindfulness can be secular or practised as part of a faith, especially Buddhism. It can help you to reach aspects of yourself that have been buried under your workload and daily worries. It produces the kind of calm that you often experience when visiting a church or cathedral. You don't have to be religious to have that experience. Practise gratitude. No matter how difficult our lives, we can all find things to be thankful for. Your friends. Your house. Your family. Your pet. Your health. However, challenge yourself if you find yourself feeling guilty because you 'should not' be anxious, depressed or stressed as you have so much to be grateful for. Mental ill-health, just like physical ill-health, can affect anyone, irrespective of their personal circumstances.

Relational self-care

The COVID-19 pandemic taught us that isolation can have a detrimental impact on our mental health. We depend on physical and social interaction for our wellbeing. For all that we are surrounded by staff and pupils during the day, teaching can be a lonely occupation. The quality of teaching and learning is our responsibility when the pupils enter our classroom and we close the door behind us. If we are suffering from stress, anxiety or depression, our perspective on how we are doing as a teacher can become distorted. We can then distance ourselves from our colleagues, ashamed to admit that we need help. We feel that everyone else can manage. Why can't we? In reality, other teachers will have their own challenges and are likely to be struggling, too.

Maintaining and fostering social relationships is vital in teaching. However much we feel that we don't have time to meet for that drink or to go out for a meal or pick up the phone, we must make time to do so. Friends and family help us to keep our perspective and to realise that we are doing our best, sometimes against challenging odds, and that our best is good enough. This is especially important if your school does not look after the wellbeing of the staff and puts the responsibility on you to look after yourself. In this kind of environment, letting off steam and getting support might be difficult or even impossible. If the school does not sustain your need to be social, your relationships outside the school are even more important. Your connections with others enable you to give to the children and young people in your care. If you do not nurture your relationships, you will eventually burn out and have nothing to give in the classroom.

Professional self-care

The greatest barrier to ECTs taking care of themselves at school is lack of time. Try to find even a few minutes to have a hot drink at break time; to take time out to eat your lunch away from your computer, your marking, your planning. Talk to colleagues and share what has gone well. 'Buddy up' with another ECT to support one another, make each other drinks and share strategies.

One of the most important strategies, but also one of the most difficult to carry out, is to be able to say, 'No' to prevent yourself becoming overloaded. Send a respectful email or memo explaining why you are unable to carry out the instruction or task, including the impact on your health, and suggest an alternative way to complete the task or solution to it.

Over to you

Make self-care a part of your life:

Step 1: Decide which of the categories listed above is affecting your wellbeing and mental health the most. Tackle it first. Rank the remaining factors and address each in turn.

(Continued)

Step 2: Take the other four categories in turn and what strategies you are going to use to address them. Write them down.

Step 3: Choose at least one strategy that you are going to introduce into your day. Focus on that strategy until it becomes a habit.

Step 4: Work in turn through the categories until they too become habits.

Step 5: Ask someone at home or work to help you to achieve your daily goals. Being responsible to someone else helps you to keep on track. Alternatively, use your diary or journal to create a supportive dialogue with yourself, ensuring you practise self-compassion.

References

Belbin (n.d.) The Nine Belbin Team Roles. Available online at: www.belbin.com/about/belbin-team-roles/ (Accessed 28 March 2021).

Butler, L.D., Mercer, K.A., McClain-Meeder, K., Horne, D.M. and Dudley, M. (2019) 'Six domains of self-care: Attending to the whole person.' *Journal of Human Behaviour in the Social Environment*, 29(1): 107–124.

Hewett, V. (2019) *Making it as a Teacher: How to Survive and Thrive in the First Five Years.* Abingdon and New York, NY: Routledge.

Lexico (2019a) Well-Being. Available online at: www.lexico.com/en/definition/well-being (Accessed 27 November 2020).

Lexico (2019b) Work-Life Balance. Available online at: www.lexico.com/en/definition/work-life_balance (Accessed 27 November 2020).

Thom, J. (2020) *Teacher Resilience: Managing stress and anxiety to thrive in the classroom.* Woodbridge: John Catt.

Quigley, A. (n.d.) The confident teacher. Available online at: www.theconfidentteacher.com/ (Accessed 28 March 2021).

Yusuf, B. (2020) 'Managing your wellbeing' in *The Chartered College of Teaching* (ed.), *The Early Career Framework Handbook*: 173–81. London and Thousand Oaks, CA: Sage.

SECTION THREE
LEARN WELL

13

HOW TO CREATE RESOURCES FOR WELLBEING ACTIVITIES WITH CHILDREN AND YOUNG PEOPLE

Becca Faal

What?

Many of the activities and resources designed to use with children and young people are written and created by adults. But what could happen if your setting worked collaboratively with the children and young people to support them to design and create resources for your setting?

Let's start with a definition:

> Co-production emphasises doing things 'with children' as opposed to doing things 'to children' or 'for children'. It is a strengths-based approach, which recognises that all children, young people and their families have their own sets of skills, knowledge and experiences which they can bring to the table.
>
> (Aked and Stephens, 2009: 2)

Creating resources with children and young people can bring many positive outcomes, including:

- Bespoke resources tailored for your school community.

- A group of engaged children and young people who have learnt more about wellbeing, worked as a team and learnt that their voice matters.

Whether you are the pastoral care lead, primary teacher or have a tutor group that you meet with each day, this chapter can work for you. You may already have a group that you work with, but may not have taken the next step of enabling them to create resources. This will help you to do this.

This chapter will give you a short overview of the benefits of co-production. It will focus on working with children and young people to create resources. You will learn about practical ways to work with children and young people to enable them to be active participants in the process. It will guide you through how to get started, what you need to consider, and give you a practical step-by-step guide on how to work with the children in your setting.

Why?

Many resources on wellbeing and mental health are created by adults for children and presented to them to use and interact with. In your setting, there may be a number of reasons why you have used off-the-shelf resources, created by adults. You may have been told by senior management that this is the programme you have to follow, you might feel that you do not have time to work with children and young people to create something, or you may just not know where to start.

Research by Aked and Stephens (2009) has shown that there are four main benefits to co-production work:

1. Higher child wellbeing

2. Increased staff wellbeing

3. A better service

4. Improved community relations

This chapter will guide you on working with children and young people using co-production techniques. I have encouraged you to start small and scale up; once you start working in this way, you will soon see benefits under these four categories in the project that you run.

In the following section I will examine four reasons why we might like to think differently and work with children and young people to enable them to create resources.

1. Children can play an active role in their education and also of those around them. Piaget's (1972) famous statement that children are not 'empty vessels' is widely accepted in education. They build their own knowledge and theories of the world based on their own actions, interactions and observations and play

an active role in enhancing their own and each other's wellbeing. If they are given the right tools and encouragement to do so, we can support them to create resources which can be used by them and others in the school.

2. During the time I spent studying for my MSc in Anthropology of Children and Child Development, I found this perception of the world very useful:

   Geertz (1984: 275) stated that anthropologists 'were the first to insist that we see the lives of others through lenses of our own grinding and that they look back on ours through ones of their own'.

   As adults, our perceptions about what children and young people want and our understanding of their lived experience of childhood will not be the same as the understanding of the children and young people themselves. We should allow them the opportunity to work together to create resources that are tailored to them and their experiences.

3. Schools are reflective of the culture and community within which they are situated. By working with a group of children and young people to create whole school resources, these will be tailored not just to the right age groups but also to the local setting. These will reflect the community's diversity, interests and culture.

4. Children often talk with each other about their wellbeing. In a study by the NSPCC (Allnock and Miller, 2013), friends were the second highest group to whom children made a disclosure of abuse. They can influence each other both positively and negatively. If children have co-produced resources, they will learn in the 'doing' and this will result in them having a greater knowledge around wellbeing and being better equipped to help themselves and their peers.

How?

I have found the most useful resources to learn more about children's participation have been written by the National Youth Agency, under the name 'Hear by Right' (National Youth Agency, n.d.). These are underpinned by article 12 of the United Nations Convention on the Rights of the Child, which has been summarised as:

Every child has the right to express their views, feelings and wishes in all matters affecting them and to have their views considered and taken seriously.

(UNICEF, 2017: Article 12)

The *Hear by Right* resources include a self-assessment tool and training on the subject.

In 2019, I co-created a set of resources, centred on safeguarding and wellbeing, for the Church of England. I worked with 90 children and young people aged from 3–18 years across a range of different groups and settings. When creating and running these groups, I used the following step-by-step process as set out below; I hope that it is helpful for you to use in the school you work in.

Think about how much time you have with the group and how many times you will be able to meet with them. This will determine how quickly you go through the steps. You can decide how long and how often you meet with the group. You should aim for at least twenty minutes per session in order to achieve a useful resource. I have included four sessions in the suggested plan below; this is adaptable depending on your setting and how long the group has been working together.

Before you run the group

Planning

Make a plan of how you will start and which group you will work with. It does not have to be complicated and it is best to start small, learn from the group and scale up when you are ready. Start with established groups in the school to support and communicate with children. These will vary depending on your setting and your role in the school, but could be a children's council, tutor group, youth parliament or nurture group.

Your role

Think about the role you will play in the group. This may vary from session to session and will also depend on the individuals in the group and your existing relationship with them. Klein (2001) identified seven roles a leader could play in a group, which Kirby and Gibbs (2006) later adapted (see Table 13.1).

Table 13.1   Facilitation roles within participatory projects (adapted from Kirby and Gibbs, 2006)

Non-directive						Directive
Abstainer	Observer	Enabler	Activator	Informer	Instructor	Doer
Leave children alone.	Reflect and feed back to group.	Encourage inclusion. Provide resources.	Challenge ideas to encourage idea development.	Suggest ways they can develop ideas.	Tell the children what to do and how to do it.	Take action on behalf of children.

In the first session you may well start off by being an instructor, but by the end of the sessions you may have moved to enabler or observer. I found that I also varied from group to group between enabler, observer and abstainer.

First session

One way of starting sessions is to begin with a game which encourages working together and participation. A game I have used a number of times is the 'egg transporter game' – see below. Alternatively, you may choose for the group to come up with something to start off with themselves.

Instructions for game

Ask the group to get into teams and give each team the same materials and an egg.

Tell them that they have a variety of materials (paper, newspaper cardboard, string) to use to stop the egg breaking when it is dropped from a height. Give the groups a time limit. At the end of the allocated time, each group should take turns to drop the egg from an agreed height. The winner is the group whose egg does not break.

Set boundaries

You will need to work with the group to set some rules and boundaries. For this part, you may need to be in 'instructor mode' to ensure that the group includes everything. Alternatively, with an older, more experienced group that has worked together before, you may be an 'observer'. It is important to make sure that the group is clear about boundaries and confidentiality, and that you are following your school policies around safeguarding.

Second session

In this step the aim is to look at the skills of the group and how they can share them to work together. This may take some time so that you ensure that everyone is included and valued. There are lots of ideas around games to share the group's skills, and to build trust and confidence. The time you take on this step will depend on the cohesiveness of the group and how long the group had been working together before you started this process. In the co-production groups that I have run, I used the following game for this step.

Activity description

The group are given pieces of paper which they then stick on each other's backs with tape. Ask the group to write a positive skill, characteristic or attribute for the person onto the piece of paper on their back. Consider playing some music while they do this activity.

The paper is then given back to the owner and they have a chance to read the positive comments written about them and to share as they wish.

Third session

Idea creation

In this stage, the aim is to have a creative session. Here you can look at what is in place already around wellbeing in your school, what they think about it, what they like and what ideas they have to create something themselves. Talk with the group about how they want to do this. It may be that they want to make a film, some artwork, making a board game, or drama. You may want to plan this before the session so that you have the right resources available.

Creating the new resource

From the ideas creation you may need to support the group as an 'advisor' to hone these ideas down to one or two to develop and create. You will then be able to move into an 'observer' or 'enabler' role while they create the resource. You may need to repeat this session a number of times to get a finished resource to then disseminate.

Final session

Dissemination

In the final session, work with your group as an 'enabler' to support them with the communication of the project and sharing of the resources they have created. In your setting, there will be a range of options that the children and young people should be familiar with. This may include assemblies, tutor time, displays. They may wish to make a short film about what they have done and how the resource can be used.

Over to you

- What do you want to achieve? Write down a few sentences to summarise your overall vision for working with children to create resources on wellbeing.
- What steps do you need to take to achieve your vision? What are the timescales for these steps?
- Who else do you need to involve?

References

Aked, J. and Stephens, L. (2009) Backing the future: A guide to co-producing children's services. Available online at: https://neweconomics.org/uploads/files/d745aadaa37fde8bff_ypm6b5t1z.pdf (Accessed 4 March 2021).

Allnock, D. and Miller, P. (2013) No one noticed, no one heard: A study of childhood disclosures of abuse. Available online at: https://learning.nspcc.org.uk/media/1052/no-one-noticed-no-one-heard-report.pdf (Accessed 4 March 2021).

Geertz, C. (1984) 'Distinguished Lecture: Anti Anti-Relativism.' *American Anthropologist* 86(2), new series: 263–278..

Kirby, P. and Gibbs, S. (2006) 'Facilitating Participation: Adults' Caring Support Roles within Child-to-Child Projects in Schools and After-School Settings.' *Children & Society*, 20: 209–222.

Klein, R. (2001) *Citizens by Right: Citizenship Education in Primary Schools*. Save the Children and Trentham Books: London.

National Youth Agency (n.d.) Hear by Right. Available online at: https://nya.org.uk/hear-by-right/ (Accessed 27 March 2021).

Piaget, J. (1972) *To Understand Is To Invent*. New York: The Viking Press, Inc.

UNICEF (2017) A Summary of the United Nations Convention of the Rights of the Child. Available online at: www.unicef.org.uk/rights-respecting-schools/wp-content/uploads/sites/4/2017/01/Summary-of-the-UNCRC.pdf (Accessed 4 March 2021).

14

WELLBEING — WHAT SEMH SCHOOLS, PRUs AND APs DO REALLY WELL, AND HOW IT CAN HELP ALL SCHOOLS

Adele Bates

What?

Pupil Referral Units (PRUs), Alternative Provisions (APs) and Special Schools supporting Social, Emotional and Mental Health issues (SEMH), by default, have to get wellbeing right. The wonderful (or terrifying) thing is, that if they don't, you tend to know about it a lot more quickly and obviously than in mainstream – the thrown desk, pupils on the roof, supply staff entering at 8am and leaving at 8.16am. And that is why shared practice between mainstream and alternative forms of education can be a fruitful exchange and mutually beneficial for pupils and staff.

In this chapter, I will outline the different considerations these learning environments must make when it comes to staff and pupil wellbeing, and suggest some ways in which this practice could benefit mainstream schools. For ease, when referring to the collective, I will call these alternative settings.

To focus the chapter, and save it becoming a book of its own (at the moment), I will focus the lens on four topics, to be approached simultaneously – safety, relationships, team, individuals – explaining why each of these approaches is so vital in alternative settings and how these can help support wellbeing in mainstream settings.

Why?

In Alternative Education we find ourselves supporting some of the most challenging learning needs that pupils have – whether that's due to disabilities, behavioural needs or circumstances. As such, our ability to adapt and differentiate is paramount, and if we don't have the right professionals on hand to support, things can go awry very quickly. It's no coincidence that staff turnover can be an issue in many of these places.

On paper, it can sometimes appear straightforward – very small class sizes, high 1-to-1 ratio, fewer obligations to stick to examination stipulations, more freedom with curriculum and delivery. And yet, the majority of pupils are a mixture of the following: disadvantaged background, on Educational Health Care Plans (EHCPs), part of or experience regular violence and aggression, have or have had dangerous home lives, have been taken away from biological parents for their own safety, are involved in illegal activity – both on- and off-site, flit between care homes, are in and out of court – for themselves or incidents they are involved in – are part of gangs, have suffered extreme abuse, neglect and trauma or have severe mental health issues and are linked with children's mental health services for self-harming, suicide attempts, etc.

Every child in your class has a high profile need – and they're all in one classroom together – hence why good alternative settings have a lot to teach mainstreams about emotional safety, inclusion and wellbeing. When we get it wrong, the consequences can be dire.

Firstly, in Alternative Education we see the individual. There is no point trying to create a lesson plan, school ethos or strategy for a class without considering an individual's needs and strengths within the collective – that way we know what safety looks like, we create the team that's required to do that, we build useful, positive relationships that will establish trust and emotional safety – so that each individual has the opportunity to thrive with their education.

How?

Safety

Safety looks different for everybody.

For one pupil, a locked door can trigger memories of when they were trapped in a room, left for days without food, with no way of contacting the outside world. For another, a locked door can make them feel safe that nothing bad outside can get in, as they remember that shutting the door meant they didn't have to listen to the adults arguing.

Safety for you will not be the same as safety for each of your pupils. Sometimes in mainstream, we baulk at the word, as if it is too strong; 'but of course they're safe' we think. For some of the pupils, you may be right, in which case, substitute the word 'safety' with the phrase 'best learning or working environment'; most physically abled people can sit at an uncomfortable desk chair for a while, but is that the 'best learning or working environment'? How much easier could I access the learning if I were physically comfortable? Then think mentally, emotionally; the morning you have an argument with your partner or housemate, do you do your best teaching? Or if you think you've left the gas on, can you concentrate as well on class 2FR's timetabled revision lesson? It is the same for our pupils.

For those for whom you do have to use the word safety, how will you know what safety looks, sounds, feels, smells and tastes like for them (I particularly mention the senses here, as autistic pupils, for example, often have a more heightened awareness to senses than their neuro-typical peers).

You have to ask, listen and believe – but of course before you do that, the pupils need to trust you, they need to have formed a relationship with you that shows you care; you also need to know how they can communicate with you – it's rarely a straightforward conversation in alternative settings.

Relationships

For most of the pupils I have worked with in alternative settings, you cannot take for granted that they have a history of being around trustworthy or safe adults. This usually presents itself in a few different ways on first meeting:

Some will tell you exactly where to go with as many four-letter words as possible – avoiding: 'It's safer for me to keep you away from me because then I am safe, you won't ask questions I can't answer, you will forget about me and I can stay in control of myself and my environment. I have learnt that if I'm aggressive people don't want to be around me.'

Some will blank you – avoiding: 'Adults can't be trusted, people in my life leave me anyway so why should I invest in you only to be disappointed again?'

Some will cling to you – attention seeking: 'I feel lonely and want to be close to someone; I haven't learnt how to do this appropriately, but I can see you're showing me interest and I want more of that. I don't want you to forget me, so I must stay with you as much as possible.'

And of course, combinations of these.

For staff to build positive relationships with pupils who do not have established patterns of positive relationships in their history, a huge amount of patience, understanding and seeing what's-going-on-behind-the-behaviour is needed. As child therapist Frédèrique Lambrakis-Haddad explains, it may be the very pupil who you find the hardest to be around, who needs you the most (Bates, 2021).

Additionally, we may well be the only safe adult in the pupil's life – checking in with them regularly, letting them know you are there – even when they've ignored you for the seventy-third lesson – could be the most important contact they have. Some safeguarding disclosures can be described as 'coming out of the blue' from staff who feel they aren't that close to a pupil; for the pupil with unsafe adults in their life, the relationship they have with school staff may be the closest.

Teamwork

Working with pupils who have experienced trauma, abuse, neglect, or who are affected by mental health issues, can be exhausting. On Twitter, I collate my #Insultoftheweek – where my community share the witticisms that our *cherubs* come up with – but day after day it can be draining. We're human, too. In addition, the pupils may well be projecting their own frustrations and challenges onto us – sometimes treating us as if we are the problem, when in reality we are more likely to be the closest person at the time.

How well staff support each other in alternative settings can make or break a place; I have, unfortunately, seen it go both ways. There is no place for 'oh but they're fine with me'. It's all hands on deck for doing what's best for the pupil, even if sometimes your own ego has to take a step back; there is a pupil who, for whatever reason, is triggered by you or your lessons, and sometimes you must pass on moments when you are not the right person to deal with it – and yes, deal with your own sense of failure instead.

The infrastructure of that support is also important. In alternative settings, we are often supporting pupils who are in therapy, and those therapists receive compulsory supervision in order to do their jobs (they're not allowed to practise without it). Good alternative settings follow this model and offer regular, scheduled supervision models – individually and in groups. This is *not* about performance or appraisal. It is about supporting the staff with the sometimes challenging situations they face on a day-to-day basis, some of which may be triggering for the staff themselves. Some alternative settings have locked doors, a lot of noise and aggression – amidst the hilarity and magical breakthrough moments. These can also affect staff, depending on their life experiences. You may have overlooked Chapter 4 (Staff safeguarding and supervision – Lessons from COVID-19 and beyond) in this book, thinking it is not relevant to you; I would urge you to go back and engage with it. Supervision is for everyone.

In addition, the communication about pupils between staff can make the difference between a good day and having to call the police – again. So, regular check-ins between all staff about a pupil's experience of the day is vital.

Every staff member needs to know where they can go for support with a child or for emotional support for themselves, both within and outside of school. Emotional health and wellbeing are a part of our daily vocabulary for our vulnerable young people, and so we must role model and practise that same care with one another. The result can be miraculous. Alternative settings are places where teens who have never read a word pick up a book, where a child who has missed seven years of education finds a talent for history, or a pupil scared of talking to new people manages to deliver a speech, because they know they are safe and supported, because this is in the very fabric of the school.

Individuals

We meet every single new person as a new human being.

One with their own needs and strengths. We spend time getting to know them, their quirks, joys and terrors – so that differentiation is never an academic thing placed on top of a lesson plan, but is the very place from which we start. If a child's just gone into respite foster care at the weekend, they may not remember the last chapter we read on Friday afternoon; the teacher will account for that. The teaching assistant gets a call that the pupil didn't have breakfast; we provide it before we attempt to teach them quadratic equations. Or we know that an autistic pupil's special interest topic is *The Littlest Pet Shop*, so we spend time learning about it ourselves and finding a way to teach chemistry through it.

In mainstreams, of course, there are more pupils and seemingly less time. Therefore, it is useful to create regular check-in activities and build-in opportunities for pupils to bring themselves and their life experiences into the classroom. 'Free Writing' is an excellent tool for this and something I advocate strongly to support wellbeing, academic progress and relationship building.

Over to you

Think about your class, your school, a particular pupil or even member of staff who needs support; that person could even be you. Choose one of the four foci (safety, relationships, teamwork, individuals) – you may benefit from going through this with a mentor or colleague:

- Which focus have you chosen?
- Which person/group of people have you chosen?
- What do you want to achieve?
- Write down a few sentences to summarise your overall vision.
- What is the first step to make this happen?
- From where do you need support?

References

Bates, A. (2021) *"Miss, I don't give a sh*t": Engaging with challenging behaviour in schools.* London: Corwin.

15

CREATING A NEW REALITY —
MAKING WORDS MATTER

Mark Goodwin

What?

There is a typed message on the wall of the workshop in the local garage where I get my car serviced – 'Your most unhappy customers are your *greatest source of learning*.' Unsurprisingly, with an ethos like this, it is a great place to take my car – they remember your name, they are honest about your car and if they can save you money they will; this is the reason why I have remained a loyal customer for over ten years. Since I first saw that sign, I have adopted it as a kind of mission statement for the work that I do with young people – of course, as educators we like to hear the feedback from happy young people. But how much more might we learn if we were brave enough to listen to the feedback of those young people for whom education, school or schooling is far less positive?

I regularly work with students who have been excluded from school and although there are lots of different reasons ultimately for their exclusions, all the young people can articulate when and how school became an unhappy place for them. They say they were:

- Treated with suspicion and treated differently.

- Shouted at ... a lot.

- Criticised, questioned and often punished for relatively minor things.

- Laughed at, mocked and humiliated.

- Told they were unteachable and shouldn't be in this or that school.

The great majority of children you work with will not be at risk of exclusion, but many of them will be thinking the same thing. They just keep their feelings hidden. But we can use these feelings for our greater good. This chapter will explore why they are feeling like that and how to turn their negative talk into positives. Turning their whole life around can be a daunting task, but turning around a thought or a sentence is totally possible.

Why?

Although exclusion is the most extreme consequence for unhappy young people, there is an epidemic of unhappiness in schools – young people in the UK regularly feature at the wrong end of happiness/wellbeing and mental health league tables. This is going to be even more of a feature in the near future whilst young people navigate the effects that lockdown has had on their life and education. As much as we are trying to steer away from using the words 'lost, catch-up, missing, behind', that may be what the young people in your life may be thinking at the moment. But to create a positive future for the next generations, we need to flip their thinking using their own words to create more positive mindsets and language.

Too often, decisions in schools are made that are for the good of the school; if just a bit more work was done to help young people to support their own wellbeing, we would have happier kids and a happier school would take care of itself.

How?

This chapter has been written after listening to the voices of young people who are unhappy with school, teachers and education in general. These aren't the words of every young person in the country, but the examples of the advice I regularly give to unhappy young people recorded below might connect with some unhappy young people you know. In my experience, if any unhappy young person implemented just two or three of these pieces of advice, they would start to move their wellbeing in a positive direction, one small step at a time.

School is boring

Try this with a student who says schools are boring, pointless or irrelevant; 'Schools provide you with the opportunity to find your meaning and purpose.' Explain that, for sure, there are constraints and limits in a school context as to what this can be but, broadly speaking, schools will help young people to develop the skills and gain the knowledge that move them closer to what they really, really want to do in life.

School and employment

Try this with a student who doesn't see the link between school and employment: 'School will help you to make sense of your future'. Explain further that, virtually from the outset of school life, school will talk about a career. Take this opportunity to start with your strengths and your interests and the subjects you are good at and see if this translates into a career. If nothing else, commit to keeping your options open and staying in education.

Lack of confidence

Try this with students who lack confidence or struggle with grades: 'Schools can be very competitive places, but the most useful competition is with yourself.' Explain that the best place to be for any student is somewhere between high expectations, competition and real self-improvement. Look after your wellbeing by trying to be better every day, even if it is just 1% better.

Anxious about grades

Another conversation with students who are anxious about or overwhelmed by grades is about balance. Try this: 'Your wellbeing will be maintained by finding balance in lots of different areas of school.' You can give examples such as individual success against the school community as a whole; the balance between academic subjects (including core subjects) and creative subjects such as art, music and sport; the balance between time with your friends and study time; the balance between using your phone and leaving it alone.

Criticising teachers or peers

When young people criticise teachers or their peers, remind them that 'It is important to work on your relationships with teachers, other young people and most importantly with yourself.' Explain that teachers are committed to student success; it is part of all teachers' job descriptions and for many teachers it is much, much more – it is a vocation. So, protect these relationships. If a relationship is damaged, can you repair it? Are you able to give second chances to teachers and peers … to yourself?

Mistakes

Too many young people have an unhealthy relationship with mistakes. Talk to them honestly about mistakes and remind them that, as a teenager, they will make plenty of mistakes. Instead of feeling guilt or shame, encourage young people to take ownership of more mistakes than they excuse; taking ownership will help them to learn from the mistake, then there is less chance of them repeating it.

Work is too hard

When a young person says the work is too hard say: 'When teachers challenge you, they are trying to help you get out of your comfort zone to a place where you can learn something new. Start by accepting this challenge and work with the support available to you – What can you do for yourself? Can your friend help you? Can you refer to a book? How can the teacher help?' Reminding young people about the sense of satisfaction from completing something difficult or something they thought they couldn't do is a great boost for their wellbeing.

Crisis of confidence

Try saying this to a person who is having a crisis of confidence: 'It is completely normal for a teenager, like you, to be plagued by self-doubt and sometimes, at critical points, you may have a crisis of confidence. These are times when your wellbeing may wobble.' Remind them that their potential is unlimited and while they remain connected to teachers, school and, most importantly, their meaning and purpose, a hopeful and bright future is always available to them.

Feeling overwhelmed

With a student who is feeling overwhelmed and close to catastrophising school, try saying something like: 'Your past shouldn't limit you and your future should not overwhelm you. Your potential is unlimited but the foundations of your future are built in the here and now so ask yourself what you can do today, right now, to take a small step in a positive direction.'

Blaming others

For a student who is quick to blame others, try a conversation about responsibility. Explain that responsibility is liberating – elaborate on this by explaining that it might not feel liberating when you are 14-years-old, but 'owning' what you do is building the independence and resilience that support a balanced wellbeing.

Paid to go to school

If a student says they should be paid for going to school ask them: 'why would you add a commercial and transactional veneer to what remains a wonderful opportunity for personal growth?' Point out that school is the last time anyone from outside your family will really care about you as a fellow human being rather than an employee and encourage them to connect with school through curiosity and self-improvement. If they really push the 'getting paid' line, remind them that their earnings increase exponentially the longer they are in education.

School is unfair

If a student says that school is unfair, really surprise them and agree. You can say that 'school life is far from perfect, because it is full of human beings trying to work at their best … and mistakes get made. However, don't get attached to those mistakes, whoever makes them. Instead, the most generous thing you can do for yourself and your wellbeing is to follow the golden rule – treat others how you would like to be treated yourself.'

Angry and frustrated

If a student is clearly angry and frustrated, try saying nothing for a while. When the time is right, ask some questions and listen. If it is the right thing to do, try talking about 'Controlling the controllables' – explain that no matter how angry or frustrated they get, they can't make other people act in a different way, let alone a way that suits them. However, they personally can make a different choice; see things from a different point of view; alter their course of action … and respond rather than react.

Commitment

Try asking what a young person is really committed to – is it being right? Is it being first? Is it being the best? Or is it trying to be a better version of themselves? This is another balancing act that will have a massive impact on their wellbeing.

What do they stand for?

Try asking what a young person really stands for. School will provide many opportunities to be kind and generous, including whole days or weeks dedicated to these attributes – will they take them? If they do, it will work wonders for their wellbeing. Furthermore, encourage them to embrace the opportunities to be of service to the school community – be a prefect, monitor, buddy or mentor.

Overwhelming

Sometimes, schools can be overwhelming – they are very busy places, sometimes chaotically so. Encourage young people to make the most of quiet time in lessons or elsewhere in the school day to just pause, be still and notice.

Really encourage young people to keep a sense of perspective and keep in mind the bigger picture of their life; there is very little that happens in school that is ever truly catastrophic, no matter how unhappy you might be at the time. Ask them to see the best part of school and be grateful for that.

Over to you

- Who are your most unhappy customers?
- What message are they trying to send you?
- What message can you flip back to them?

16

EXPLORING CHARACTER AND SUPPORTING WELLBEING WITH FRIDA KAHLO AND ALBERT EINSTEIN

Frances Corcoran and Selena Whitehead

What?

Teachers around the world are under immense pressure to prepare their pupils for a fast-changing global landscape, which requires developing 21st-century skills and meeting exacting academic targets. In addition, businesses around the globe repeatedly call for young people with perseverance, resilience and motivation.

Within the unpredictable challenges and adversity that life throws at us daily, it is critical to remember the importance of strategies to support good mental health and wellbeing. Schools are also rightly concerned with the behaviour of their cohort and strategies to deal with it. All schools have their own values, and instilling these in a meaningful way across their body of students takes explicit practice and action.

What connects the so-called soft skills needed for 21st century work – wellbeing, positive behaviour strategies and values? Character! Introducing the language of character to the entire student body is crucial. By doing so, the building blocks for these very different challenges can be built.

So, how do we embed character strengths into the very heartbeat and fabric of school life?

To help facilitate this, we use stories of global game-changers: amazing people who have achieved the extraordinary. Their stories demonstrate the vital role that character strengths played in their lives.

For example, Frida Kahlo's story is one of resilience, courage, and creativity. Helen Keller teaches us about gratitude and perseverance, and Martin Luther King Jr. is an extraordinary example of optimism and integrity. Understanding the role of character in these remarkable people's lives is the first step in recognising the role it can play in our own lives.

All of us face challenges and difficulties in our lives. By actively developing key character strengths such as optimism, gratitude, resilience, perseverance, adaptability, kindness, creativity and tolerance, we can develop the coping strategies to thrive and flourish, increasing the mental health and wellbeing of students and staff.

We'll show you easy ways to incorporate these stories and character strengths into the curriculum.

Why?

Those of us working in education are keenly aware that character, personal development, and wellbeing provide the stepping stones to flourishing as human beings, and never more so than now.

Universities, business leaders, and parents all speak of the need for improved mental health in our young people. Having the means to help support their mental health helps them thrive, whatever path they choose to take.

Schools that have embraced the language of character and explicitly built character strengths have seen improvements across the board, both in behaviour and wellbeing. This needs to happen across school life: from assemblies to tutor time, from the playground and school corridors to individual subject classes. It needs to be brought into conversations with parents, student assessments, and homework. In other words, it needs to be truly embedded into all facets of students' lives.

Consistently emphasising the language of character increases students' vocabulary and self-awareness, allowing them to not only reflect on their behaviour and attitude more effectively, but look ahead with greater understanding and perception.

Our vision involves a clear, consistent message: identifying what character means in practice and understanding how developing character can benefit wellbeing.

For the former, schools are encouraged to reward character strengths they see in action. For instance, perseverance is recognised when a student completes a difficult maths challenge, courage is acknowledged when a shy student raises his/her hand to ask a question, and kindness is commended when a student helps a classmate without being asked.

This reinforcement of behaviour with language is far more beneficial than a generic 'well done for trying hard'. Building on this by helping students fully understand and appreciate the correlation between character and wellbeing can have lifelong benefits. For example, allowing creativity to play a role in our lives boosts the endorphins that improve our wellbeing. Incorporating optimism when approaching tasks and activities increases positivity, and taking a position of gratitude when considering who and what we have in our lives leads to contentment.

Providing inspirational stories, along with the tools and language to enable students to develop their wellbeing, can prove invaluable and life-changing.

How?

Schools spend considerable time deciding on their values. To bring these values to the fore, each school requires a dedicated, co-ordinated approach. Helping students recognise the values that their school embodies through the stories of amazing historical figures can be the link many need to 'make it real'.

Exploring the story of an amazing person can be transformational for students' understanding of character. The realisation that they can share some aspect of their life with an awe-inspiring achiever builds their sense of identity and wellbeing. Classrooms are diverse places with students from different backgrounds and situations. Seeing themselves reflected in the life of someone who went on to do incredible things can be inspirational.

There are many different aspects of a person's life that can become the touchstone for helping them relate to that person. Stories of people who moved to a new city or country at a young age, suffered prejudice or discrimination, or struggled to learn to read can all be inspirational. Seeing that amazing person first as accessible and relatable, and made 'amazing' by their character strengths, shows us how we can all flourish and thrive, no matter what the circumstances.

Again, it is key that schools reinforce this understanding of character across the fabric of the entire school. This can be achieved in a variety of ways:

Assemblies

Leading the entire school through a series of assemblies on amazing people focuses everyone's minds for that week. Assemblies are an ideal way to highlight the given values and beliefs of the school. Reinforcing those values through the stories of amazing people brings to life the virtues you wish to instil. For example, if a school has resilience as a key value, then using an assembly to discuss Frida Kahlo can be powerful. Learning about her childhood polio, her tragic accident and her ensuing physical setbacks is a graphic way to discuss the importance of bouncing back from adversity. Relating how resilience is essential to our wellbeing can be a key message across the school years. Communicating that everyone has suffered setbacks and difficulties, including those we think are amazing, can be empowering.

It's not a question of never failing at anything, but of understanding how we can learn from those 'failures' or setbacks, pick ourselves up, and carry on. Sometimes resilience requires us to dig deep and press on. However, sometimes resilience asks us to demonstrate adaptability – to try a different route to achieve the same goal. Again, if the language of character is embedded, these messages become increasingly relatable and meaningful.

Tutor time

Using form or tutor time to discuss character and wellbeing is ideal. Taking just ten minutes out of the day to allow students to consider the life of a person who achieved something amazing, looking at their strengths, and reflecting on how this can help their own wellbeing, is enormously important and can add something different and very valuable to the school day.

For example, the following quote that is commonly attributed to Abraham Lincoln, though of uncertain origin (Quote Investigator, n.d.), can encourage a discussion on optimism: 'We can complain because rose bushes have thorns or rejoice because thorn bushes have roses.'

This can lead to teacher-led discussions and activities and explore current approaches to challenges. For example:

- Discuss what benefits there are to changing those approaches.

- Consider the benefits of a positive mindset.

- Debate which other character strengths can play a role in developing optimism – such as adaptability, gratitude, and perseverance. Discuss how these can be brought into the classroom.

- Recognise that whilst there are roses this does not diminish the reality of the thorns – do we need gloves or shears to cut away at the thorns?

Teachers can also discuss the reality that Lincoln was brought up in a poor family, did not go to school and learned to read only of his own volition. Regardless, he rose from very humble beginnings to become the 16th President of the United States.

Blended learning

Blended learning, when combined with homework, provides the opportunity to bring discussions around character and wellbeing into the home, reinforcing the consistency of language introduced at school. It encompasses the whole community in the school values. Schools can ask that students research a given character before a certain lesson, extending this learning by asking them to identify different character strengths demonstrated. For example, before studying the Crimea War, students could be asked to find out about Florence Nightingale and Mary Seacole. How did they demonstrate optimism, tolerance, kindness, perseverance, and initiative?

Students could also be asked how to develop key character strengths for their own wellbeing. Ideas for doing this might include creating a 'protective shield' made up of everything that helps them bounce back when they are feeling low; writing down and learning a positive mantra to repeat to themselves when needed; writing a letter to someone to maintain a relationship; practising gratitude in a daily diary; writing a song or rap about something that makes them feel positive.

Over to you

How could you implement these ideas in your school and community? Think about what makes your school and community unique. How could character strengths work improve the wellbeing of everyone, encouraging the thriving and flourishing of all?

What steps do you need to take to achieve your vision? What are the timescales for these steps?

- Use real-life stories of amazing people to bring to life the character strengths they demonstrated. Assemble them into a diverse collection that can resonate with your students on different levels to develop their identity and support their wellbeing.
- Decide when and how in the school day you want to promote character and wellbeing. Assembly; form time; subject classes; personal, social, health and economic (PSHE) education; or homework, all provide good opportunities.
- Introduce character and the story of an amazing person into learning experiences. For example, amazing scientists can introduce character at the beginning of a science lesson. Consider using the start of every lesson to set the expectation for character development: 'Today I'm looking for you to work collaboratively and with enthusiasm.'

Reinforce the message of character and how it impacts on wellbeing around the school. Make character the foundation for expectations of how students should participate and interact within the school community.

References

Quote Investigator (n.d.) We Can Complain Because Rose Bushes Have Thorns, or Rejoice Because Thorn Bushes Have Roses. Available online at: https://quoteinvestigator.com/2013/11/16/rose-thorn/ (Accessed 29 March 2021).

17

SOCIAL AND EMOTIONAL LEARNING — CIRCLE SOLUTIONS AND ASPIRE

Sue Roffey

What?

Most of the time, students in school are learning knowledge and skills, such as those in the English and STEM curriculum. Although these subjects are important, education needs to be more than this if young people, their families and society are to thrive in the future. 'Learning to Be' and 'Learning to Live Together' were highlighted by the Delors Report for UNESCO (Delors, 1996: 37) and have been re-affirmed by the OECD Learning Framework 2030 (OECD, 2018). Social and emotional learning (SEL) is the umbrella term used internationally for these important pillars of learning.

SEL is one of the seven pathways to wellbeing identified in the Australian Scoping Study on Approaches to Student Wellbeing (Noble et al., 2008). But for SEL to be effective, it needs to be a safe, enjoyable and supportive experience for both students and teachers, take place regularly and the learning reinforced in everyday interactions. The ASPIRE pedagogy addresses these issues within the Circle Solutions (Roffey, 2020) framework. This chapter will clarify why SEL matters, what ASPIRE stands for and how it works, and give examples of Circle Solutions in practice across the world.

Why?

We are living in a time when the world has gained much in knowledge but little in wisdom. We can put a human being on the moon and develop a vaccine to protect us against COVID-19, but have more broken families than ever, deteriorating mental health for many, continuing racism, misogyny and homophobia and a belief that the more things you accumulate the happier you will be. Authentic wellbeing, however, lies in the quality of our relationships, the extent to which we feel positive about ourselves, other people and the world around us and being able to find meaning and purpose in our lives.

Many young people struggle with their mental health, and this has been exacerbated by the pandemic, which has brought uncertainty, anxiety, loneliness and feeling out of control for many. It is more essential than ever that schools focus on the protective factors that promote resilience. These include feeling connected with others, learning to understand and manage emotions, and appreciating that there are alternative ways of thinking, being and doing. SEL is not only a way of developing personal and inter-personal skills, it also gives pupils a framework to explore attitudes and perception. This ranges from giving students responsibility for developing a friendly and inclusive learning environment to reflecting on wider social issues of racism, toxic masculinity and evaluating social media.

There is also evidence (Durlak et al., 2011) that regular SEL can raise attainment levels, as students are more likely to be positively engaged with school.

How?

There has been a well-founded critique of SEL (Ecclestone and Hayes, 2009) that when students are invited to discuss emotionally sensitive issues, this might open Pandora's box, where students do not feel safe and teachers feel unprepared to respond effectively. The ASPIRE pedagogy has been developed and used for more than a decade to ensure that SEL does not mirror therapy. There is evidence of positive outcomes across the age range (Dobia et al., 2014, 2019; McCarthy and Roffey, 2013).

Circle Solutions is not a programme, it is a framework for delivering curriculum content intended to be:

- interactive: pupils do things together

- discursive: students talk about important issues

- reflective: pupils are encouraged to think through issues themselves

- experiential: many activities are game-based, giving students the option to think through alternative ways of being and doing.

Teachers choose activities most appropriate for their class and the age they are teaching. Circle sessions need to take place a minimum of once a week but more often if possible. Regularity is more important than the length of each Circle. A principal of a school in the US once told me that 'Magic Circles' took place for twenty minutes after recess every day in every class. He said they had transformed the culture of his school.

There are commonalities between Circle Time and Circle Solutions but also significant differences, specifically the ASPIRE pedagogy. Here, we give a brief rationale for each letter in this acronym and an example of how each works in practice.

A is for Agency

Self-determination is a cornerstone of wellbeing. This means not being controlled by others but being able to make your own decisions. Students are not told what to think or given the 'right answer' but offered opportunities to work out ways of being and doing. Circle Solutions empowers students and gives them a voice. Alongside agency comes responsibility.

Let's look at an example of Agency in practice. Students are given a hypothetical scenario such as a new girl, Lily, arriving in class. No one is unkind to her but no one speaks to her much either. She doesn't know what to do. Small groups are asked to discuss the following:

- What would you be feeling if you were Lily?

- What would you want to happen?

- What could we do to make Lily feel welcome here?

- What words would we say to her?

This activity forms the basis for a class response to a new entrant – they have already worked out how to do this.

S is for Safety

Healthy relationships are physically and emotionally safe. Safety is maintained in Circle Solutions by two of the three guidelines. There are no 'put-downs' and each pupil can choose to 'pass' if they wish. There is no pressure to say anything. Students discuss issues, never incidents, and they do that in the third person (someone) rather than the first (I or me), using hypotheticals and role-play. Safety is also maintained by doing activities in pairs and small groups.

Here's an example of Safety in practice: The Strengths in Circles cards (Deal and Roffey, 2015) have seven statements for each of the six ASPIRE principles. The ones for Safety are:

- We are kind in what we say and do.

- We build trust with each other.

- We look out for each other.

- We can get help.

- We forgive each other.

- We are reliable and honest.

- We learn from our mistakes.

In small groups, pupils are given one of these cards. They are asked to discuss the following:

- Does this happen in our class?

- How would we know if it was happening, what would we see, what would we hear?

- What would people be feeling if it was happening?

- What is one thing we could do to make sure this happens?

Students then report back to the whole Circle.

P is for Positivity

Rather than focus on problems, Circles Solutions is strengths and solution-focused. Pupils discuss what is already working well and how they could build on this. Many activities are presented as games and this is important for motivation. Having fun together is one constant feedback from pupils. Pupils laughing together releases oxytocin, the feel-good neurotransmitter that bonds people together and increases trust and collaboration.

Here's an example of Positivity in practice: Strength cards are laid out in the middle of the Circle. Students have been mixed up and are in pairs. Each picks up a strength they have observed in their partner and tells them why they have chosen this.

I is for Inclusion

Feeling you belong, you matter and that you can contribute is a major protective factor in resilience and wellbeing. Pupils play games that mix everyone up so that pupils regularly talk with those outside their usual social circle. In pair-share activities they find out what they have in common. This enables people to get to know each other, which over time reduces prejudice, intolerance and bullying behaviours.

An example, raising the importance of belonging:

All pupils mingle together in the middle of the Circle until the facilitator calls out a number. Students quickly congregate in groups of that number. This happens several times with different numbers. Participants are then asked to reflect on and discuss in pairs the following:

- What did it feel like to be included in a group?

- What did it feel like to be looking for a group?

- What did it feel like to be left out?

R is for Respect

One of the guidelines encompasses respect in asking students to listen when one person is speaking. Verbal contributions are kept short so that no one can dominate. The other way in which respect is demonstrated is acceptance and the avoidance of judgement. Although some contributions might not seem appropriate, the teacher simply nods and says thank you. Respect applies to individuals but also to cultures.

An example of Respect in practice: A wide range of photos or symbols cards are spread across the Circle. Students are asked to pick up a card that is something they are proud of in their community. In groups of three or five pupils say why they picked up that card and explore what they might have in common.

E is for Equity

This has several dimensions. The first is that everyone has the opportunity to contribute and, for some individuals, that may mean being flexible or providing some support. Importantly, the facilitator – usually a teacher – is a full participant and does everything that the students do.

Here's an example of Equity: Young children work in pairs or small groups to share whether or not a selection of scenarios are fair or not, e.g. 'Jack has been playing on the bike in the playground for over ten minutes and Farah wants a turn. He keeps saying "in a minute" but won't get off.' Is this fair? What might happen to make it fair?

The activities for SEL are many and varied. Paired interviews and pair shares enable students to find out about each other and what they have in common. These small group activities are often preceded with a game to mix everyone up. Hypothetical scenarios and role-play give pupils the opportunity to discuss issues in a safe place, creative activities stimulate conversation, as do photos, symbols cards, strength cards, video clips and pictures depicting emotion. Whole group games connect to each other and are often energising and fun. There are many resources to support SEL, although some may need some tweaking to fit with the principles.

Circle Solutions have been evaluated in several studies that show that this intervention is effective in developing a happier, safer, class climate and promoting a sense of belonging amongst participants. Teacher-student relationships also often change for the better.

Quotes from research studies

'I like knowing about other people more.' (McCarthy and Roffey, 2013: 48)

'I try to understand how other people feel and think.' (Dobia et al., 2014: 9)

'You can go to AGC (Aboriginal Girls Circle) sad and you'll leave it like really happy.' (Dobia et al., 2014: 8)

'I have learnt to be more confident with myself and not to put myself down.' (student) (Dobia et al., 2019: 86)

'Children seem to include special needs children more in classroom life.' (teacher) (Dobia et al., 2019: 81)

Over to you

These questions may guide you in getting SEL on the agenda in your school.

- What might students be dealing with in their lives and how does this impact on their learning, behaviour and mental health?
- What is currently in place for students to support each other and to boost their resilience?
- Do we believe SEL needs to be a wellbeing priority in our school?
- What are the first steps in making SEL a reality and how can we ensure there is protected time for this?

References

Deal, R. and Roffey, S. (2015) *Strengths in Circles Cards: Building Groups that Flourish and Fly.* Geelong: Innovative Resources. Available to purchase from: https://innovativeresources.org/resources/digital-applications/strengths-in-circles/ (Accessed 29 March 2021).

Delors, J. (1996) *Learning: The Treasure Within.* UNESCO Publishing. Available online at: https://unesdoc.unesco.org/ark:/48223/pf0000109590?posInSet=12&queryId=f9897ad1-e31b-4acf-a2d8-e64997ad28ab (Accessed 29 March 2021).

Dobia, B., Bodkin-Andrews, G., Parada, R., O'Rourke, V., Gilbert, S., Daley, A. and Roffey, S. (2014) *Aboriginal Girls Circle: enhancing connectedness and promoting resilience for Aboriginal girls: Final Pilot Report.* Sydney: Western Sydney University.

Dobia, B., Parada, R., Roffey, S. and Smith, M. (2019) 'Social and emotional learning: from Individual skills to group cohesion.' *Educational and Child Psychology*, 36(2): 79–90.

Durlak, J.A., Weissberg, R.P., Dymnicki, A.B., Taylor, R.D. and Schellinger, K.B. (2011) 'The impact of enhancing students' social and emotional learning: A meta-analysis of school-based universal interventions', *Child Development*, 82(1): 405–432.

Ecclestone, K. and Hayes, D. (2009) *The Dangerous Rise of Therapeutic Education.* London: Routledge.

McCarthy, F. and Roffey, S. (2013) 'Circle Solutions: a philosophy and pedagogy for learning positive relationships. What promotes and inhibits sustainable outcomes?', *International Journal for Emotional Education*, 5(1): 36–55.

Noble, T., McGrath, H., Roffey, S. and Rowling, L. (2008) *A scoping study on student wellbeing.* Canberra: Department of Education, Employment and Workplace Relations (DEEWR).

OECD (2018) *The future of education and skills: Education 2030 – the future we want.* Paris: OECD. Available online at: www.oecd.org/education/2030/E2030%20Position%20Paper%20(05.04.2018).pdf (Accessed 29 March 2021).

Roffey, S. (2020) *Circle Solutions for Student Wellbeing* (3rd Edition). London: Sage.

18

TAKING THE STRESS OUT OF EXAMS FOR STUDENTS

Sarah Brazenor

What?

As educators, we know that exams do not suit every type of learner, but they are a part of our education systems, for better or worse. This chapter will introduce you to ways to support your students who find exams stressful.

Exams can be stressful for students and this can greatly affect their ability to shine in their subjects. Although we will be using the term 'exam' in this chapter, all the suggestions are applicable to students taking exams, tests and assessments throughout their school life.

In this chapter, we will explore the common reasons for stress and what we can do to help our students overcome it. We will discuss the importance of confidence, preparation and truly tapping into their natural learning ability. We will show how understanding how you learn and how to revise in the right way can reduce exam stress. In addition to this, we will touch on the methods that can be used by students to reduce stress. We will look at techniques such as breathing, exercise, essential oils and emotional anchors that help the student feel in control, calm and confident.

Why?

Exam stress can have the following effects: poor exam results, poor sleep, feeling unwell, panic attacks, not eating, anxiety around being at school. This can lead to a lifelong phobia of exams and/or being in school. Often students can start to feel a failure and not good enough.

Imagine your best student, who always does well in class, falling to pieces in an exam and even leaving the examination room having written very little, if anything. They feel a failure and there's nothing you can do to help them. Saying they'll be okay isn't enough, and you see their confidence drop and their love of your subject wane. It's heart-breaking.

By understanding what is driving that fear of exams, you can begin to implement the changes that student needs to succeed. It may be they don't know how to revise, it may be they have a fear of the examination hall, or they may not know how to answer the questions. By going through the steps in this chapter you can begin to see where to target your support. With the right support and actions, your student can really achieve what they are capable of and the exam stress just slips away.

How?

It is important not to assume that everyone's exam stress is caused by the same thing. We can never assume to know how someone is thinking, so it's really important to identify the reasons for the anxiety in order to support the student in the best way for them.

Below, I share a three-step plan to help alleviate exam stress in our students, followed by a suggested action plan you can implement for your students.

Step 1: Identifying which students need your help

Identifying what is upsetting the student is perhaps the best place to start. Often the reason may surprise you; listed below are the top five reasons that come up time and time again.

1. Fear of failure

2. Fear of the exam hall

3. Not being able to revise

4. Thinking they can't do exams

5. Not believing they are clever enough

Sometimes the language that teachers, parents or peers use can greatly influence a student's ability to remain confident when faced with exams. Let's look at some common statements:

'You haven't got long to revise.'

'These are the most important exams of your life.'

'I know you can do better.'

This type of 'motivational' language seems to increase as students go further up the school years, partly due to the perceived importance of the exams and the pressure on schools to hit targets.

Our younger students may not even be aware they are taking a 'test' but for those who develop anxiety around testing at an early age, it's important that we help them overcome this fear as early as possible.

To summarise this step

1. Identify the nervous/stressed students.

2. Identify what they are nervous about.

You might find it useful to produce a checklist of questions to ask students, to help dig into their thinking and feelings around exams and have this as a resource to refer back to.

Step 2: Reframing their identity-level thinking

Once you have identified the right students and the reasons for their exam stress, we can start helping students re-define their thinking. For the purpose of this step, we will look at two most common thoughts:

- I'm a failure.

- I'm not clever enough.

These are what we call identity-level statements and the individual truly believes this is who they are. It's very important to change this deep-level thinking. The key thing for turning around this language is helping the student see their own brilliance and helping them see they have the power within them to overcome their particular obstacle.

Lack of self-belief is the biggest hurdle to students overcoming exam stress. If we can change their perception of themselves and their ability, they will grow in confidence and the reasons for being stressed about exams will disappear.

It is also important to mention that low self-belief in their ability may well be hidden from view. Your student may appear not to be bothered by their results, or be the 'class fool' to try and distract you from the real cause. However, every behaviour has a purpose, even if it's not suitable classroom behaviour. In fact, it's probably even more important if you see a disruptive student, or one that struggles to stay focused, that you ask yourself 'What is this about? Could it be hiding a bigger problem?'

If you suspect a student has limiting beliefs, I suggest the following steps to reframe these deeply-held beliefs

Adding the word 'yet' to a negative statement adds in the possibility that change is possible. So, for example, 'I can't do maths' becomes 'I can't do maths, yet'. As you can see, the second statement is full of the possibility that things can improve. Another example could be, 'I don't like exams' becomes 'I don't like exams, yet'. The second statement gives you the possibility that things may change.

If adding the word 'yet' isn't possible, then 'because' is another powerful word. 'I can't do that test' – because? Using the word 'because' really helps dig into the beliefs of the brain. You can keep asking 'because' until you get to the root cause of the belief. It can take time and your student may get frustrated, depending on how old they are, but it's a great technique to dig deeper without the student feeling they are being counselled.

Below is a true-life example of how such a technique could work with an 11-year-old student:

'I can't do that exam'

Because?

'It's too hard'

Because?

'I can't write fast enough'

Because?

'I'm slow'

This student actually did need more time to complete the exams, and by having that extra time, the stress slipped away and their true ability began to shine.

It's easy to fall into the trap that someone isn't trying hard enough, but actually, a stressed student is usually one that is frustrated at their own ability and wants to do well.

Step 3: Environmental and capability changes

Once you see that a student is beginning to understand and address their reasons for exam stress, it is possible to suggest some environmental and capability strategies to them. These are often what are proposed in the first place, but without changing the identity-level thinking, these can just be short-term fixes.

However, if you are confident that you have their core identity-level thinking and feelings identified, then now is a good time to look at implementing the following.

1. Exercise before a test

This is a well-known technique which increases the level of endorphins. These are often known as the 'happy hormones' and, by doing gentle exercise, the body begins to relax, and stress levels decrease.

Exercise should be taken up to twenty minutes before an exam in any of the following forms:

- Walking to school

- Cycling to school

- Ten-minute jog

- Ten minutes of skipping

- Walking for twenty minutes

- For our younger students, games like 'catch the ball', hopscotch or a general play outside would be helpful.

The idea of this type of exercise is not to get out of breath and give the heart a workout, but more to relax the body and give the mind time to release those hormones.

2. Hydration and fuel

When a student is suffering from stress, it's more important than ever to make sure they are properly hydrated and have eaten.

Many schools do a breakfast club in exam weeks, but for those that don't, making sure students have water and suitable snacks will make a massive difference to their concentration. For our younger students, it is a good idea to invest in some healthy snacks that you are able to give out in the break before they have a test. For example, you could have a fruit bowl in the classroom or some savoury snacks that students can pick from. This would be a great experience to introduce our younger students to the importance of snacks before exams, which they can take with them through their school journey.

3. Breathing

Breathing is the single most important technique we can teach our students. When we are stressed, we breathe quickly and shallowly. This reduces the amount of oxygen going into the blood stream, which in turn can affect our concentration and focus.

The key thing to calm an anxious student is to count the breaths and to breathe out for longer than you breathe in:

- Breathe in for a count of four, hold for a count of two and breathe out for a count of six. This gives your conscious brain something else to focus on and the stress and anxiety will start to disappear.

- Count the breaths taken. This has a great calming effect. Again, counting the breaths allows the conscious brain to calm down. They may then be able to move to counting breaths in and out.

- Nose and Mouth. Some students might be able to focus on breathing in through the nose and out through the mouth. Again, it's all about focussing the mind on something else rather than panic.

4. Emotional anchors

Depending on the age of the student, positive anchors could be beneficial to alleviating stress. Anchors are used a lot in improving emotional stability and would justify a book in their own right; this is a simple introduction to this topic.

Here are a few examples:

- Favourite pencil case

- Lucky socks

- Tissue with favourite essential oils added – e.g. lavender, mint, rosemary

- Drops of essential oils can be added to clothing, which can be smelt whilst doing breathing exercises

- Scented rubbers

Over to you

Below is a framework you can adopt to help reduce exam stress in your students.

Step 1: Identifying the right students and what could help them straight away

1. Who do you think may be experiencing or could develop exam stress and anxiety?

(Continued)

2. Check with all members of staff that interact with your students, as they may behave differently in different situations. This is especially important for the students that may well be masking their worries and limiting beliefs.
3. What are their 'I' statements?
4. What strategies can you put in place immediately?

Step 2: Longer-term planning

Short-term changes can have a positive impact and break the negative cycle, but now think about what can be put in place longer term to prevent issues resurfacing.

1. Introduce the concept of negative talk and beliefs in lessons and assemblies. Identifying what students are thinking about themselves will help educate the whole class or year group.
2. Decide how often you are going to check with students how they are feeling. Every half term would be the recommended time scale to start with.
3. Track your progress for each student. Perhaps get them to do a reflective diary about how they are feeling so you can monitor and highlight the improvements to them.

To carry out the action plan, it is important to identify the member of your team who will be implementing it. It is also important that the action plan is shared amongst all colleagues working with the student. Reframing thinking can be done more effectively if everyone is conveying the same message to the student.

Time must be put aside to discuss the plans for each student for the very best results.

It is perfectly possible to reduce exam stress very quickly with the right reframes and a consistent approach from your team.

SECTION FOUR

ENGAGE WELL

19

RELATIONSHIPS AND SOCIAL CAPITAL

Sue Roffey

What?

Relationships are the crux of both our happiness and our misery. When they go well they support us through the tough times and enhance our lives by sharing the good times.

There is now a good deal of evidence to say that the quality of the learning environment in a school is about the level of social capital (e.g. Glasgow Centre for Population Health, 2013). Social capital, as a concept, has changed meaning over time, but many commentators now refer to this as 'the quality of relationships across an organisation or community'. Do those relationships build trust, support, confidence, collaboration and wellbeing, or do they leave people walking on eggshells and watching their backs? Does it matter if you are in the 'in-crowd' or do you fear that you will be bullied or at the very least undermined by being put down and marginalised? The opposite of high social capital is a toxic environment – which is not good for anyone's wellbeing.

This chapter will cover the importance of positive relationships as a foundation for wellbeing in a school and the vision that promotes that alongside the micro-moments of interaction that build a positive culture. We give examples of good practice and ideas for action.

Why?

The way people feel about being in school, both students and staff, is largely dependent on the relationships they experience there. What someone feels about themselves makes a difference to both motivation and actions.

- A feeling of being valued promotes cooperation.
- A feeling of being cared for enhances understanding and compassion.

- A feeling of being respected promotes respect for others and willingness to listen to them.

- A feeling of being included raises commitment and motivation.

- A feeling of fun relieves stress and fosters belonging.

- A feeling of belonging builds resilience.

- Feeling good improves creative problem-solving abilities.

All of this promotes caring communities, but importantly it also facilitates learning. A young person struggling with adverse childhood experiences (A.C.E.s), such as neglect, deprivation or family conflict, may not feel that school is for them. They may not see themselves as successful learners in a competitive environment and don't fit in because their strengths are not acknowledged or their voice heard. Negative outbursts may be quickly punished. Rather than school being a place of refuge, kindness, predictability and support, it becomes somewhere to be simply tolerated or even feared.

When schools acknowledge the centrality of relationships this will inevitably impact on behaviour policies and practices in schools. Those that focus primarily on rewards and sanctions make little allowance for context, feelings or relationships. Such approaches attempt to change behaviour from the outside in, and are likely to have only short-term impact. Building positive relationships attempts to change behaviour from the inside out so that pupils begin to choose pro-social behaviour as this brings feelings of worth and connection (see also Chapter 8 by Mark Goodwin for more ways to improve relationships through building connection). For children and young people who have experienced trauma and other embedded difficulties this may take time, and teachers need both emotional and practical support to keep going. When teachers are in a supportive culture they are more likely to deal effectively with challenges.

According to Putnam (2000), there are two kinds of social capital. 'Bonding social capital' brings people close together and might be seen as the glue of connection, whereas 'bridging social capital' reaches out to others. The former risks exclusion, where only those who 'fit' and obey unwritten rules are accepted. Bridging social capital enhances inclusion and is flexible and respectful in its interactions, rather than saying 'this is the way we do things round here – take it or leave it'. It values all stake-holders and gives everyone a voice. Sometimes these dimensions of social capital are referred to as 'inclusive' and 'exclusive' (Roffey, 2013). Inclusive environments honour everyone.

How?

Although relationships across a whole school create the overall culture, this comprises conversations and interactions across different parts of the system: school executive with staff; teacher-teacher; teacher-student; students with each other and home-school. Although not all are addressed here, much can be applied across boundaries. As Bronfenbrenner's ecological model shows (2009), there is bi-directional influence between each, and changes occur over time. What is said in the staffroom, for instance, will impact on what happens in the classroom and in meetings with parents, because relationships are driven by belief, perception and attitude, not just skills.

Relationships are enacted in the micro-moments between people. It is what is said and how it is said that constructs culture. This cannot be left to chance as it will often be the negative that dominates. As one teacher said in a research study (Roffey, 2007: 21): 'To have any sort of racist comment or other negative is not acceptable. We build an acceptance of others, all are different but all have a place.' Strengths-based language gives people positives to live up to. The following acronym sums up some of the important micro-moments of interaction (Roffey, 2016). These apply across a school setting.

Going WALKIES: Some micro-moments of interaction

W: Welcome: A sense of belonging is a critical component of wellbeing and resilience – so making people feel their presence matters by just saying 'Hi, good morning, how's it going' can be a powerful message of welcome, especially if accompanied by someone's name. How people both begin and end their time in a school shows how people are valued. This can be enhanced by giving new members of staff a supportive mentor for a few weeks to help show them the ropes and settle in – and ensuring everyone who leaves has a good send-off.

A: Acknowledgement: Just a simple 'I noticed that …' makes a difference. It stops people feeling their efforts are taken for granted. Gratitude, e.g., saying thank you to a colleague, a pupil or the person who cleans your classroom, changes culture. Acknowledgement also means noticing when someone is a bit down and perhaps needs extra support.

L: Listen: Time-poor teachers find it hard to listen well, but giving full attention for 20 seconds may be enough to make someone feel heard rather than dismissed. Listening is more than eye-contact, it includes asking questions to clarify understanding and perhaps not interrupting or giving advice! Active listening is respectful and can boost almost any relationship which is why it needs to be taught as part of social and emotional learning.

K: Kindness: Random acts of kindness are as beneficial for the giver as the receiver. One school has a 'Kindness Board' in the staffroom where people stick post-it notes to acknowledge random acts of support. A kind word is as easy as a sharp one and takes no more time. Another school has 'This is a No Put Down Zone' poster in every corridor, classroom, staffroom and office. Everyone knows what it means. When asking students about bullying in the school they pointed out that this didn't happen because of this 'no put down' thing!

I: Invitation: This could be making space for others to join in a conversation, or asking for their opinion. Occasional whole staff social functions, perhaps including friends and families, enable people to get to know each other outside their specific role. This can lead to broader conversations and greater collaboration.

E: Enthusiasm: When someone has achieved something, giving them the credit with genuine warmth impacts on everyone. Active constructive responding has been shown to be one of the major factors of a successful marital relationship (Gable et al., 2004). Perhaps we can do this for each other.

S: Smile: Neuropsychology tells us that we don't only smile when we feel good, the very act can cheer us up. And it costs nothing.

And **Silence:** There are times when we need to bite our lip and not say what is on the tip of our tongue. As a general rule perhaps ask 'will it help' before putting something into words. If it won't, then don't say it.

The role of school leaders

The vision of school leaders is critical to the cultural development of a school. If a school leader believes education is to maximise the potential of every child, values staff, and has the relational skills to both communicate their vision and build a team around them, then there will be an upward wellbeing trajectory. How they model this approach matters.

I arrived early in the morning to a school in New South Wales, Australia, to interview teachers for a research project. I arrived to find the principal busy making breakfast on a barbecue for the staff and was told that this was not an unusual occurrence. This principal saw himself as a servant leader, using his authority to empower others, not to dominate. This lack of ego had a major impact on wellbeing in a tangible way – the school's sickness budget was routinely underspent.

In a large school in Essex, England, the headteacher made a point of finding out about the lives of every member of staff and so was able to ask meaningful questions about how they were doing, not just in school. When he returned from a period of sickness, the staff had put out bunting, made cakes and made it clear how much they had missed him. He had developed a culture of care by modelling what mattered.

Healthy relationships are oiled when people are given the opportunity to find out about each other and what they have in common. This needs to go hand in hand with valuing diversity.

Teacher-student relationships

Biographies are full of tales of teachers whose words of encouragement and belief in the best of someone turned lives around. The research on resilience (Werner and Smith, 2001) indicates that having someone in your life who thinks you are worthwhile can promote positive adaptation to chronic adversity. Usually these people are in families, but sometimes they are in school.

For a long time the mantra in education has been about 'teacher control'. One-sided control in any relationship is seriously unhealthy, and can lead to dominance, bullying behaviour and ultimately abuse. We need to offer an alternative to this, and model what is healthy. This means clarifying the difference between being in charge of a class and trying to control students. This does not mean condoning unacceptable behaviour but ensuring that pupils know they have choices and must take responsibility for the decisions they make, including any consequences. Teachers also have a choice – they can control the words that they say and the actions they take in any given situation. Although it is natural to apply this specifically to the teacher-student relationship, it is also applicable to other relationships between stakeholders in the school context. Table 19.1 provides a summary of what this means in practice.

Pupil-pupil relationships

There are three aspects to relationships between pupils – one is about how they are given guidance to construct a climate on inclusion in the class that ensures everyone is safe and happy; the second is having a curriculum that promotes the learning of social and emotional understanding and skills; and the third is about how this learning is embedded in everyday interactions. This is covered in more depth in Chapter 17: Social and Emotional Learning – Circle Solutions and ASPIRE.

Table 19.1 In charge or in control? (Based on Roffey, 2011)

Caring and in charge	Controlling	Example of practical application
Supporting	Criticising	How can I help?
Encouraging	Blaming	Tomorrow is another day, let's try again then.
Listening	Complaining	What happened – what did you want / expect to happen?
Accepting	Nagging	That didn't go well. How can we make it better next time?
Trusting	Threatening	I will come back later and see how you are doing.
Respecting	Punishing	The decision is yours – but these are the likely consequences of what you choose.
Negotiating difference	Bribing, rewarding to control	Let's see if we can both get what we want here.

Over to you

These questions might guide you in exploring relationships in your school and identifying the steps that might be taken to build a community of care that maximises engagement, wellbeing and learning.

- What is your school's vision? What are the priorities?
- Who believes that the quality of relationships matters for learning and wellbeing?
- What are you already doing that works, and how might you build on this?
- What professional development is in place, and how might that be followed up?

References

Bronfenbrenner, U. (2009) *The Ecology of Human Development: Experiments by Nature and Design*. Cambridge: Harvard University Press.

Gable, Shelly L., Reis, Harry T., Impett, Emily A. and Asher, Evan R. (2004) 'What do you do when things go right? The intrapersonal and interpersonal benefits of sharing positive events.' *Journal of Personality and Social Psychology*, 87(2): 228–45.

Glasgow Centre for Population Health (2013) Briefing Paper 38: Social Capital and the Wellbeing of Children and Adolescents. Available online at: www.gcph.co.uk/assets/0000/3818/BP38_Final.pdf (Accessed 22 February 2021).

Putnam, R.D. (2000) *Bowling Alone*. New York: Simon and Schuster.

Roffey, S. (2007) 'Transformation and emotional literacy: the role of school leaders in developing a caring community.' *Leading and Managing*, 13(1): 16–30.

Roffey, S. (2011) *Changing Behaviour in Schools: Promoting Positive Relationships and Wellbeing*. London: Sage.

Roffey, S. (2013) 'Inclusive and Exclusive Belonging: The impact on individual and community wellbeing.' *Educational and Child Psychology*, 30(1): 38–49.

Roffey, S. (2016) Going WALKIES: The micro-moments of supportive school relationships. Available online at: https://growinggreatschoolsworldwide.com/going-walkies-the-micro-moments-of-supportive-school-relationships/ (Accessed 22 February 2021).

Werner, E.E. (2013) 'What can we learn about resilience from large scale longitudinal studies?' in Sam Goldstein and Robert B. Brooks (eds), *Handbook of Resilience in Children*: 87–102. New York, NY: Springer.

Werner, E.E. and Smith, R.S. (2001) *Journeys from Childhood to Midlife: Risk, resilience and recovery*. New York, NY: Cornell University Press.

20

PURPOSEFUL PARENT ENGAGEMENT

Kelly Hannaghan

What?

This chapter will outline my journey and experiences of building strong home school connections to grow positive wellbeing cultures in education. I will highlight why parental engagement is such a vital component for any whole school wellbeing strategy, and how the process of working collaboratively with parents/carers can dramatically improve resilience through relationships. I will share the simple step-by-step process I have used to implement purposeful parent empowerment groups, which have resulted in greatly improving both the learning and living outcomes of children and young people, enabling them to thrive through life's adversities. We will also explore how to overcome any challenges in implementing parental engagement programmes.

Why?

Before I outline the importance of parent/carer engagement, I invite you to reflect on the risks of not building positive home-school links. How would that play out in your school community? What would be the consequences for pupil wellbeing and attainment and how would the relationships between staff and parents/carers be impacted?

I have worked with many schools and settings in supporting the development of building whole school approaches for positive mental health and wellbeing. I have seen how impactful wellbeing is when put at the heart of a school; it changes cultures and enables communities to thrive.

By focussing on parent/carer engagement and offering them a voice and role to play in growing and sustaining positive outcomes for wellbeing, this becomes a sustainable and successful intervention tool.

Starting from where people are

The first experience for a parent/carer bringing their child into school may be a daunting one. Parents/carers often unknowingly carry their own educational experience into the school environment (Peña, 2000). These learning experiences may be shrouded in negativity and fear and this will affect the emotional space that they are functioning from.

Human beings often carry concerns around feeling judged (Simmons, 2020) and not being socially accepted. An example of this is 'cliques on the playground' where parents/carers may not feel a sense of belonging. This can manifest into avoidant behaviours, especially if parents/carers feel internally threatened.

Another example is the parent/carer 'wearing of the mask'. This is when parents/carers attend the school environment with an emotionally guarded 'mask' or 'painted face' to show everything is just fine and that they are emotionally in control of themselves; this may not always be the case, but is seen as the accepted norm to fit in with the parent/carer community. This is an emotive safeguarding technique that many of us use in order to give the impression that we are 'fine', but that I noticed more in school playgrounds than in other settings. These organically grown protective factors can certainly have a negative impact on happiness that flourishes from self-validation and authenticity.

The purpose of pulling together fragmented communities

I have seen first-hand how segregated school environments can be, due to the lack of cultural understanding. This can be particularly challenging for parents who have learning needs. Schools can be seen as intimidating and competitive cultures.

My work in parent engagement has created outstanding outcomes for children, their families and schools. A south-east London school had been placed into special measures by Ofsted (the Office for Standards in Education, Children's Services and Skills in England) and all relationships in the school had broken down; all trust was gone. Now was the time to rebuild this school with parents/carers, by working on trust and a sense of purpose. My mission was clear: I wanted to put relationships at the heart of the school.

I was invited to be part of a school improvement plan, which quickly established that building new strong relationships was the way forward. This was the space where my innovative *Family Matters* programme evolved.

This was an empowerment group for parents/carers to collectively come together, to be a force for change and to collectively build a successful parent support network. The results were phenomenal and included parents and me being invited to the Houses of Parliament to participate in a round-table event and share our journey.

Bolster community spirit in challenging times

I will never forget the joyous moments of seeing a primary school culture change before my eyes. Families who were previously visually segregated within the school playground were now coming together and there was a new sense of hope and community spirit developing before me. Gone was the cultural, financial or intellectual divide; people were coming together with a new sense of hope. Families were supporting each other with their new-found common language of empathy and kindness. Relationships between teachers and parents/carers improved, and a shared understanding and consistency of language started to thread through every fabric of the school community.

The outcomes for pupils were outstanding. This was supported by the consistency of approaches and a shared responsibility for emotional health that was used both within school and at home. Together, the school community became stronger and more resilient.

How?

Start with a clear vision and action plan. Set yourself clear goals. Provide knowledge-driven strategies to support parent/carer empowerment and build positive relationships by providing learning skills and resources that recognise the importance of emotional health.

Help parents to explore the risks around mental illness for themselves and their families; provide them with the tools to recognise the symptoms of depleting mental health and empower them with effective strategies so they develop a sense of agency over how to respond to their individual needs.

Below, I outline the key steps I have taken when implementing successful parent engagement and empowerment strategies.

Build relationships to break down barriers

- Offer coffee mornings in a mutually supportive environment so that you are able to offer parents a voice.

- Gather information from parents/carers for desired topics of discussion.

- Be visually present on the school playground at the beginning and end of each day, offering emotional support and guidance.

Parent evaluations

- Think about the questions you would like parents to answer.

- Create your questionnaire, ensuring it is accessible and inclusive for all, e.g., braille, audio, digital and paper-based. It may be helpful to offer one-to-one meeting spaces to complete these questionnaires in a safe and non-threatening environment.

- Send out the evaluations with a deadline date for return.

- Collate and analyse parental/carer responses.

- Produce a synopsis of outcomes for all stakeholders.

- Embed the feedback from the evaluations into purposeful actions that feed into the sessions.

Create/build purposeful workshops for wellbeing

- Use the information from the evaluations to create your agenda for workshop events.

- Produce and share a calendar of events and topic areas.

- Secure a time and space to hold these events whilst always keeping the school and parents/carers informed.

- Consider using a variety of communication methods to invite parents/carers to the sessions, e.g., notice boards, school website, letters home, social media platforms, designated private groups and face-to-face contact.

- Develop a contract for parents/carers to sign, which outlines the safe and confidential environment in which you will facilitate the workshops.

- Plan your environment for parents/carers, ensuring it is a welcoming and safe space – tea, coffee and biscuits are a must.

Planning your content

- Create content that is relevant to the parents'/carers' needs, based on the evaluation responses.

- Each session should last around 1.5 hours and should include time for a check-in at the beginning of the session and check-out at the end. For example, you could start the session by asking them to reflect on their week's celebrations and to consider how they have overcome any challenges. At the end of the session, you could ask what learning they will take from the session and what action they plan to take as a result.

- It is crucial to the review process that each session builds upon areas of discussion from previous sessions.

- Create a session feedback form to ascertain how helpful the session has been for parents/carers. Ensure there is a space to highlight recommended improvements, not just successes. This ensures you offer every participant a voice that matters, and this information will feed into your future planning processes.

Your first session

- Meet and greet parents/carers in your designated welcome space.

- As part of that process, explain the importance of safe boundaries e.g. confidentiality, safeguarding, taking turns to speak and the importance of listening to others.

- Ensure the message that they are responsible for their own wellbeing is clear.

- Set out the aims and objectives of the session and the plans going forward, e.g. where and when future sessions will be held (you may want to consider offering 6-week blocks of sessions).

- Provide some time for Q&A at the end of each session.

- Create and distribute feedback forms. You can use this feedback to inform the focus for your next session.

- Manage the session effectively: keep track of time boundaries and manage heightened emotions, should they arise. Mutual respect for all is key.

Facilitator reflection time – review of first session

Protect some time at the end of the session, in a quiet, private space, to reflect on and review how the session went. The best time to do this is immediately after the session.

1. Before looking at the feedback forms, pause and consider how you felt the session went. This will allow you to catch your breath and have a quiet moment to celebrate that you have completed your first session. You may want to jot down a few notes or keep a reflective journal about your own experiences as well as those of your group participants.

2. Now read, digest and analyse the feedback forms from your parent/carer group. It is important that you make designated time for this and not just informally sift through the feedback forms as you walk out of the room; this stage is essential to building successful future workshops.

3. Embrace all feedback, regardless of its positive or negative stance. Remember, all feedback is good feedback; it ensures you build a successful programme for the needs of your group.

Facilitator reflection time – self-care, supervision and compassion

Your wellbeing in this process is absolutely vital in order for you to sustain and develop a positive impact. With this in mind, ensure you care for yourself as well as others. It is important to recognise and respond to any emotions that may have been triggered within you. This could be a great time to speak to someone or even secure some form of supervision or coaching, which in turn will help you grow and develop as a facilitator.

How to overcome challenges

You are likely to be faced with challenges along the way; these can provide useful learning opportunities. The greatest barrier I faced was engaging parents'/carers' interest at the start of the process. My key message here is to take gentle steps and start by building comfortable relationships. These valuable moments and conversations will, over time, start to develop a sense of openness and safety. You will become the person flying the flag for wellbeing support, and people will trust you over time. Remember, however, that it's important to recognise your own emotional needs, as you can't 'pour from an empty cup'. Ensure you take responsibility for your own self-care process, building in helpful habits and secure time to look after yourself.

Over to you

From my experience, the overwhelming positivity of having a purposeful parent engagement programme in your school not only has a significant impact on bringing parents/carers together, but radiates wellbeing throughout your whole school community and its families. This triangulation between pupils, parents/carers and the school is a winning formula for mental health and wellbeing for all.

(Continued)

Now that you have read my process for implementing such a programme, make some notes on how you can start the process in your school. It doesn't matter what your formal role is in school - anyone with a keen interest in wellbeing can take a lead on parent engagement. It may be that your first step will be to approach the leadership team about this.

- What is your vision for parent engagement? Write this down as a concise statement.
- Make a note of the first three goals to be added to your action plan.
- Consider what questions you will ask within a parent evaluation.
- How will you measure the outcome of your strategies for parent engagement?

References

Peña, D.C. (2000) 'Parent Involvement: Influencing Factors and Implications.' *Journal of Educational Research*, 94(1): 42–54.

Simmons, H. (2020) Feeling Judged: Parenting Culture and Interpersonal Surveillance. In: *Surveillance of Modern Motherhood: Experiences of Universal Parenting Courses*: 93–118. London: Palgrave Macmillan, Cham.

21

STAFF WELLBEING — IT'S NOT JUST FOR TEACHERS

Kimberley Evans

What?

When talking about wellbeing in schools, the focus is often on pupils and teaching staff. Your school is a unit, a family, a body of force, and every cog in it is equally important; in order to achieve whole school wellbeing, therefore, the wellbeing of non-teaching staff needs to be given the same consideration and importance as that of teaching staff and pupils. This chapter will show you why meeting the wellbeing needs of all your staff, not just teachers, is so important and give you practical steps to make positive changes for everyone. Depending on your role in school, you may not think you can have an impact on this, but whether you are a teacher, school leader, or work in a non-teaching role, this chapter will suggest ways you can be a force for positive change within your school.

Why?

Whole school wellbeing is exactly that – whole school – incorporating everyone; everyone is equally important in the common/final goal – to help pupils reach their potential. If you are only taking care of some of the staff, it won't work as well.

A survey I carried out in November 2020 with non-teaching staff across the UK showed that although 75% of respondents said that their school considered their wellbeing, 60% felt it was given less consideration than the wellbeing of teaching staff. As a profession, we have made great improvements in the field of staff wellbeing over recent years, but quite often staff wellbeing is created with mainly teachers in mind. It gets discussed at staff meetings and ideas are thrown about, but typically only a fraction of staff are at those meetings. Sometimes, a wellbeing committee is formed with only teaching staff.

Think about your car; you fill it with fuel, you clean it (maybe?), you clean out the inside. But none of those things are necessary for it to pass its regular roadworthiness test. That requires time and effort; an oil change, new tyres, getting a cracked windscreen repaired. How often have you put those little things off, only to be told that an even bigger problem – a failed roadworthiness test – has now occurred? All those little things are vital for your car to run smoothly and effectively, and they are all very different, just like every single person who works in your school is vital to how smoothly it runs and how well the pupils achieve their potential. Quite often, non-teaching staff are forgotten about with staff wellbeing because they do not have direct contact with pupils, but this doesn't mean the work they do doesn't have an impact on them.

Let's think about your non-teaching staff. List four and what each of their jobs involve on a typical day (we'll come back to that list later, keep it handy). You can see that they are all very different, but all these tasks/jobs/roles have an impact on pupils. Maybe not immediately, but over time. So, looking after your non-teaching staff is just as important as your teaching staff. What works well for your teaching staff may harm the wellbeing of your office staff, for example. In my November 2020 survey I also asked 'How do you feel support staff's wellbeing is different from that of teaching staff?' The following comments made for interesting reading:

> 'Teaching staff are the priority in most minds, they get a lot of leeway and consideration of their needs and health.'

> 'Teachers are the focus. Support staff and part-time staff to a degree feel like 2nd class/after-thought. Not included in briefings etc.'

> 'Teaching staff's opinions and wellbeing appears to be more of a priority.'

> 'It can be (but not always) an after-thought.'

Think about your staff/colleagues; how would they answer those survey questions? What thoughts might they have about the wellbeing offer at your school? A whole school approach to wellbeing needs to address everyone's needs. Let's look at ways to do this.

How?

Go back to that list of four different staff. Look at how different their roles are, how varied their day-to-day tasks are. This should highlight how their wellbeing needs will all greatly differ. When I asked on Twitter: 'How do you support the wellbeing of your non-teaching staff?', many replies were along the lines of: 'Same as for our teaching staff'. Whilst this is well-intentioned, are they meeting the needs of all their staff if they are treating them all the same? Would you meet the needs of all your pupils if you treated them all the same? A site manager does a very different job from a teaching assistant; an HR manager's day is very different from that of a deputy head.

The best approach to staff wellbeing is to adopt a bespoke approach. But before you throw this book down and say, 'I haven't got time to make individual wellbeing plans for everyone!', let me reassure you that you don't need to.

A class of thirty pupils has a vast array of individual needs. We don't write thirty separate lesson plans; we adjust, accommodate and make alterations to the main one.

We think about all those pupils and what outcome they will get from the lesson; we need to adopt a similar process with staff wellbeing.

Start with a basic plan of how you can improve things in your school and adapt, tweak and adjust it for different roles. It is not going to be a 'one size fits all' approach. You are also probably not going to get it right on the first attempt either (more on this further on).

As a starting point, you need a set of core wellbeing values that are consistent across the board, and a benchmark to work from. Be clear with your staff that these are the basics – the minimum – and that you will be building on these for specific roles to ensure there is wellbeing for all.

Your core values will be personal to your setting and environment, but should include areas involving:

- Communication

- Workload

- Adequate meal and break times

- Staffroom facilities

- Toilets

- Up-to-date equipment.

Communication

Are *all* staff included in whole school emails, or just the teaching staff? Do all staff know what is in the diary? How do you communicate with staff? Are briefings working? Is your email policy inclusive to all? (Some are so restrictive they are actually hampering flexible working strategies).

Workload

In reducing workload for some, are you inadvertently creating more for others? Are your staff leaving at a sensible time? Is all paperwork necessary and does it improve pupil achievement?

Adequate meal and break times

Do lunch duties prevent your staff from having a break throughout the day? Is workload managed well enough for staff to have a break?

Staffroom facilities

Do all staff have access to somewhere to have a break and is equipment such as a fridge, microwave, etc. available? Are there enough seats for everyone? As the COVID-19 pandemic has resulted in significant changes to shared areas since 2020, it is worth reviewing staff facilities. Have the needs of your staff changed? What adjustments can you make to communal areas so it is safe for staff to use them?

Toilets

Are there enough toilets for everyone to use when they need to? Are they in locations staff can easily access during break times? Are they inclusive to all? Are they pleasant to visit?

Up-to-date equipment

Are computers slowing people down and contributing to stress levels? Is the photocopier frequently breaking? Does the site and cleaning team have what they need to do their jobs effectively?

The above points are just a quick overview of what to consider when drawing up your core wellbeing values. Think about the setting of your school, your ethos and values, your demographics and environment. Make them work for you to get the best out of your staff.

Once these are in place, it will be time to think about the individual more. Explain to staff that, although these are your school's core wellbeing values, individuals' needs may vary slightly, so a more bespoke approach will enable everyone to be at their best and achieve their potential, just like it does for the children. Framing it like this will help them understand that it is ok to treat people differently and that certain individuals may be getting 'special treatment', because that is how you meet their needs.

I'm afraid one chapter can't provide all the answers. The specifics will relate to your particular staff and current circumstances. Think back to that list we made of different people's roles and how their days differ. Let that guide you. Don't be afraid to change things; what works this year will not necessarily work in three years' time. Here are some ideas to get you thinking:

- Supervision for teaching assistants and pastoral teams

- Screen filters for office staff who use computers all day

- Ergonomic chairs for office staff

- Subsidised work clothes for site team

- Time for a proper break for staff that cover lunch duty, e.g. time out of class in the afternoon

- Mentors for all staff

- Wellbeing buddies that cross roles/functions

- Staff socials at different times.

Involving all your staff in the process, by asking them what they need, is key to getting this right and can be done by everyone.

You can initiate change, whatever your role, by having a positive impact on the staff you work with. You can do this by being considerate of everyone's needs and thinking about how your role impacts those of others. You can advocate for staff that aren't listened to. You can support all staff with kindness, whatever your or their role is.

As part of my work in supporting staff wellbeing, I suggest schools have a wellbeing lead who is not on the senior leadership team. This encourages more staff to get involved and start talking. Starting with an anonymous staff survey allows all staff to voice their opinions and explain their needs, and provides a great starting point. They have all the answers; there is no need to take great stabs in the dark when you can simply ask them. Check in with staff frequently – consider adding a conversation about wellbeing needs into all staff performance reviews. Things change and people's needs change.

Over to you

This might sound like an insurmountable or never-ending job. It's not. You do not need to make everyone's life perfect and you don't need to try and reinvent the wheel.

If you are in charge of staff wellbeing or on the senior leadership team, my first suggestion would be to run an anonymous staff survey to all staff. You can create one yourself on Google Forms or SurveyMonkey, but using an outside provider can increase staff confidence in the anonymity of the survey and lessen the workload on you.

Then just try and change one thing for each of the different roles we spoke about earlier. Ask them the simple question: 'How can we make your work day better?' Simply asking this question can improve wellbeing as staff feel more valued and part of the team.

If you are reading this as a member of staff without responsibility for staff wellbeing, think about the members of staff you directly work with and how you can make a difference to their work days. You could make some little changes yourself that could have a massive impact on their life which in turn could help you and your pupils.

Happy staff = happy pupils

- What are the different roles within your school?
- Where do these people work and what factors affect their wellbeing?
- What simple changes could you implement to make a positive difference to their day?

22

SUPPORTING HAPPY, HEALTHY PLAYTIMES — PLAYGROUND WELLBEING BUDDIES

Thérèse Hoyle

> The ability to play is critical not only to being happy, but also to sustaining social relationships and being a creative, innovative person.
>
> (Brown, 2010)

What?

In this book, we explore whole school wellbeing in many contexts; however, there is one area of child and whole school wellbeing that often sadly gets forgotten – the playground.

In this chapter, I will outline why we need to reinvigorate our school playgrounds and how we can use Playground Wellbeing Buddies (PWB) to support happy, healthy playtimes. Finally, I will invite you to consider how you can develop wellbeing buddies in your school and playground.

Why?

In a recent conversation I had with Laura Chamberlain, Wellbeing Lead at Eastrop Infants and Southfield Junior School in England, she mentioned that, when developing their whole school culture of wellbeing, they realised that every part of the day – including lunchtimes and playtimes – needed to be included, with everyone on board. As a result, they developed a PWB team which, she said, 'transformed our playground and playtimes and boosted the self-confidence of the children'. When we think about wellbeing in schools, we need to take a systemic, whole school approach, as Frederika Roberts discusses in Chapter 1.

Sadly, playtimes can be a neglected part of the school day; although most children's experiences in the playground are positive and enjoyable, for some the playground can be an unhappy place where aggressive behaviour and bullying is experienced and/or witnessed.

Seventy-five per cent of bullying happens in the school playground (Sharp and Smith, 1992) and according to Craig et al. (2000), there is more frequent playground than classroom bullying (4.5 vs 2.4 instances per hour). Womack (2007) attributes this to breaktimes being dull, with little for children to do. In fact, in my experience, many playgrounds resemble barren prison grounds rather than inviting play spaces.

A child's feelings about school are often defined by how happy a playtime they have had; whether they had friends to play with, or their classmates allowed them to join in their games, whether there were enough activities and there was enough space to entertain them.

Many teachers will tell you that good teaching and learning time is frequently taken up with resolving disputes after lunch and, as you will know, an upset or anxious child may also find it difficult to concentrate and learn.

Play has many benefits for children, families, and the wider community, including

- increased physical health and wellbeing

- increased social, emotional and mental health and wellbeing

- strengthening and development of friendships

- improved cognitive development

- language development

- the development of confidence and self-esteem.

(Hoyle, 2021)

Creating positive playtimes is therefore vital.

How?

For over twenty years, I have been running *Whole School Positive Playtime* and *How to be a Lunchtime Supervisor Superhero* programmes and have written two books on this subject: *101 Playground Games 2nd Edition* (Hoyle, 2021) and *101 Wet Playtime*

Games and Activities (Hoyle, 2009). Through working with over 500 schools, I have discovered that one of the secrets to happy lunchtimes and playtimes lies in organising a group of students to be PWBs. Their role is to look after children who don't have anyone to play with, organise games and ensure the playground is a safe, enjoyable space for younger children. An added benefit I hear from teachers is that this role gives children responsibility, improves their social skills, increases self-confidence and builds leadership skills.

In initial conversations about PWBs, schools often tell me that they don't work. While there are many reasons why having PWBs may not work, it is possible to successfully create PWBs and turn a boring playground into a stimulating, engaging place that supports the social, emotional, mental and spiritual wellbeing of all pupils at playtime.

Useful steps to help guide you

Step 1: Playground wellbeing survey

Start by assessing the wellbeing of children at lunchtimes and playtimes and evaluate your current provision. On my *Positive Playtime* masterclass, the children fill out a playtime wellbeing audit.

Consider including questions such as:

- Are you happy at playtime?

- What do you like most about playtimes?

- What do you like least about playtimes?

- What are your favourite playtime activities?

- Is there enough to do?

- What equipment would you like to play with?

There are many excellent examples of playtime wellbeing surveys online, including on my website (Hoyle, n.d.a), so you don't need to reinvent the wheel.

Step 2: Recruitment and selection

Ideally, select the oldest age group in primary or infant schools, and 13–14-year-olds in secondary schools.

Start by talking to the students during an assembly about the role of the PWB, explaining what they will be expected to do and the qualities they will need. Reassure them that they will receive training in how to be a friend to anyone looking lost or lonely, learn playtime games to play with younger children, and most of all that they will have fun.

Place enticing posters around the school, inviting children to fill out an application form, explaining where they can obtain one. I encourage teachers to support children in filling these in.

Step 3: Interviews

The interview process is an important part of becoming a PWB and an opportunity for children to explain why they want this role and demonstrate positive social skills. It's also an opportunity to learn vital life skills. Each child is interviewed by a couple of adults – usually one of the PWB adult coaches and someone from the senior leadership team. Many schools I have worked with have been creative with the interview process and have organised the local football coach, supermarket manager or local sports person/celebrity to be on the interview panel. This has made the process a lot more exciting. After all children have been interviewed, they gather in groups and learn new playground games. This is always a popular part of the interview process, during which interviewers can observe the children's social skills, their ability to play, cooperate with others and join in with games.

Schools frequently find they have a lot more children applying than they anticipated, so set a whole day aside for this process.

Step 4: Selection

Don't assume that children with poor social skills, or those who struggle with their behaviour, are quiet and shy, or have low self-esteem are not suited to the PWB role. In my experience, when these children positively influence a younger child's life, their self-confidence is greatly enhanced.

How many children you select to be on duty each day will depend on the size of your playground and number of children in your school. Generally, however, four to six children are sufficient. If you have had large numbers of PWB applicants, you can rotate your children's PWB duty days. This is best practice also because children shouldn't be on duty every day; they need time for free play.

Responsibilities of the Playtime Wellbeing Buddies

It is important that PWBs understand what is expected of them.

Their responsibilities will be dependent on the size, demographic, ethos and the playtime management of each school. However, these are some things they may assist with or take responsibility for:

- Organising games

- Looking after younger children

- Befriending lonely children and helping them make friends

- Spotting children at the buddy bench and finding them a friend to play with or getting them involved in a game

- Taking out and putting away playground equipment

- Mediation (this involves additional training and is a skilled role).

(Hoyle, 2021: 25)

The PWB system is beneficial when properly implemented and managed but is likely to fail if these children are expected to just get on with their role without appropriate training or supervision.

Training your PWBs

Ideally a teaching assistant, lunchtime supervisor, play leader, physical education lead or teacher will take responsibility for the PWBs, their training and ongoing support. This person will have been trained as a PWB Coach and have the skills to support this group of children.

Training of the PWBs should include reiterating the importance of their roles and responsibilities in supporting younger children. Rotas and duration 'in post' should be clearly set out. Additionally, PWB coaches need to:

- Support the PWB to develop communication and problem-solving skills

- Help them learn to respect one another

- Help them identify their own strengths

- Support them in being cooperative

- Teach them strategies to understand and manage their own feelings.

I encourage you and the PWB coaches to also teach a selection of playground games. Many of the schoolchildren have lost the art of knowing how to play games, so this is a wonderful opportunity for your older children to learn and teach games to younger children. You may have books of games in school, of course, but for additional ideas, you can download a free copy of ten *Traditional Playground Games* from my website (Hoyle, n.d.b), taken from my *101 Playground Games* book (Hoyle, 2021). These games can then be given to each child and they can keep and use them as a reference.

Training your PWBs is an important step and helps contribute to a positive whole school ethos and supports the children to develop into responsible individuals with a sense of empathy, respect and care for their peers and the adults.

Supporting PWBs

Once the PWBs are active in the playground, the PWB Coach can mentor them and help them evaluate how well their games went.

PWBs love to wear a 'uniform', which distinguishes them in the playground. This may be a cap, or tabard and badge. Involve them in researching and choosing what they want to wear.

Once your PWBs have been hired and trained, introduce them in an assembly to the school and get them to contribute to 'Playground News' at weekly assemblies.

Crucially, for your PWBs to work successfully, they need ongoing support. This includes regular times for training and to talk about their experiences, successes and challenges. Ideally this should happen weekly or fortnightly.

Maximising the benefits of PWBs

Buddy bench

Many of the schools I've worked with have a 'buddy bench', which they use to address loneliness and foster friendship at playtimes. If children are upset, have no one to play with, or wish to talk about a concern they have, they can go to the buddy bench. A PWB will then come along and support them: find out how they are, help them come up with solutions to their problems and sometimes find them someone to play with or ask them to join in a game. Buddy benches foster kindness and inclusion in schools.

Establish a Playtime Wellbeing Council

This operates in a similar manner to a school council and comprises all PWBs, representatives from each class, a member of the senior leadership team and a lunchtime supervisor. The children bring playtime issues/ideas from their classes to the council to discuss and the children come up with solutions. These ideas and solutions can then be fed back to each class.

Certificates

At the end of term or their time as a PWB, children receive a certificate to thank them for their contribution and hard work. This is given out in assembly.

Over to you

The setting up of the PWB system has proved invaluable in the many schools I have worked with. I hope the outline of my process for a successful PWB system will help you create PWBs in your school.

The time and investment you spend on developing your playtimes and training up your PWBs will contribute to creating a positive whole school culture of wellbeing where children are responsible, kind individuals, who show empathy, care and respect to everyone in their community.

- Now, take some time to create an action plan, outlining the steps you need to take to develop the programme, and discuss this with your senior leadership team and staff/colleagues. Are any elements of a PWB programme already in place at your school? If so, what are they?
- What is the first step you will take to create a PWB programme in your school?
- When will you do this?
- Who else do you need to involve in the process? You may want to suggest including the PWB programme in the school's development plan – children spend approximately 20% of their time at school in the playground, yet strategically planning for this time in the school day is often overlooked.
- How will you get the buy-in of others who have a say in this?
- Did you know that, in England, you can fund development of your lunchtime and playtimes with the PE and sport premium? The revised government guidance now puts 'Active Play' (DfE, 2014: How to use the PE and sport premium) as its second priority for how the funding should be used.

References

Brown, S. (2010) *Play*. New York: Penguin.

Craig, W.M., Pepler, D. and Atlas, R. (2000). Observations of bullying in the playground and in the classroom. *School Psychology International*, 21: 22–36.

DfE (2014) *PE and Sport Premium for Primary Schools*. Available online at www.gov.uk/guidance/pe-and-sport-premium-for-primary-schools (Accessed 28 March 2021).

Hoyle, T. (2009) *101 Wet Playtime Games and Activities*. London: Speechmark Routledge.

Hoyle, T. (2021) *101 Playground Games*. 2nd Edition. London: Speechmark Routledge.

Hoyle, T. (n.d.a) Thérèse Hoyle Consultancies – Shop. Available online at: https://theresehoyle.com/shop/ (Accessed 26 March 2021).

Hoyle, T. (n.d.b) Traditional Playground Games. Available online at: https://theresehoyle.com/free-playground-games/ (Accessed 26 March 2021).

Sharp, S. and Smith, P.K. (1992) 'Bullying in UK schools: The DES Sheffield Bullying Project', *Early Child Development and Care*, 77(1): 47–55.

Womack, S. (2007) Boredom leads to school bullying. *The Telegraph*. Accessible online at: www.telegraph.co.uk/news/uknews/1565456/Boredom-leads-to-school-bullying-says-report.html (Accessed 26 February 2021).

23

DRIVING PUPIL ENGAGEMENT THROUGH THE PSHE AND R(S)HE CURRICULA

John Rees

What?

When the UK Secretary of State announced that Personal, Social, Health and Economic (PSHE) education was going to be statutory in England, I wept. The years of campaigning were finally over. Unfortunately, that was in 2008, prior to a UK general election. Subsequent administrations took another decade to acknowledge the evidence supporting the entitlement of all children and young people to statutory, high-quality health education and the multiple benefits this can bring to learning and life chances.

In England, fee-paying schools have, for a number of years, been mandated to teach PSHE. The Department for Education (DfE) decided that, from September 2020, two new subjects should be mandatory for all pupils in state-funded schools (DfE, 2019). The first, health education, now forms part of the statutory curriculum for all pupils aged 5–16. Secondary schools (ages 11–16) must now teach relationships and sex education; and primary schools, while laying the foundations of relationships education, can now also choose whether to teach sex education to support the learning that is already happening in science.

This chapter is based on the curriculum in England, and outlines how the statutory expectations of relationships and sex and health education (RSHE), sitting within a wider framework of PSHE (DfE, 2020), can contribute to improving wellbeing and attainment. The principles remain applicable to educational settings around the world.

Why?

The UK generally, and England specifically, has significantly reduced unwanted teenage pregnancies over the last two decades, but rates remain stubbornly high (Teenage Pregnancy Independent Advisory Group (TPIAG), 2010). We have high rates of sexually transmitted infections, young people's mental health is at crisis point (Public Health England, 2014), and we know that some children are targeted to engage with illegal drugs.

The need for high-quality PSHE has never been greater, and the entitlement of school pupils – some of whom are likely to live into the 22nd century – to keep themselves safe, happy and well should not be forgotten.

Despite, or perhaps because of, the pandemic, we currently have wonderful opportunities to provide high-quality relationships and health education and to harness this to improve the learning and life chances of children and young people for many years to come.

The authors of the DfE statutory guidance (DfE, 2019) could not have foreseen the pandemic, but it is spookily prescient that we now have an expectation to teach about mental health, hand washing, how germs and viruses are transmitted and the importance of vaccination, along with safe and appropriate internet use, the importance of family, respectful relationships, physical health and wellbeing, and a list of other topics.

We should not mistake this as exclusively a public health initiative. There is strong and growing evidence (Department of Health, 2012) that high-quality teaching and learning that promotes pupil wellbeing can improve attainment and academic outcomes (PSHE Education Strategic Partners Group Members, 2018).

It is easy to assume that if we simply employ scare tactics, young people will avoid the perils of adolescence and arrive safe on the shores of adulthood. It is equally tempting, and erroneous, to wheel-out the odd 'ex-user', an occasional teenage mum, or perhaps show pictures of infected lungs, in the hope that young people will immediately see the error of their ways – or more likely the errors of adults – and make safe, healthy, rational decisions about who and how they love, what and how they eat and drink, and how they engage with social media.

This is especially true if we over-focus on knowledge. High-quality PSHE should also develop pupils' skills to be able to better manage their emotions, relationships and wellbeing. Similarly, children and young people need help to foster the pro-social, pro-health attitudes and attributes that enable them to flourish. Evidence-based, engaging PSHE/RSHE can support the improvement of children's physical, social and emotional development and enhance their academic attainment to enable them to become happy, successful, contributing adults.

How?

England's schools will, inevitably, be at different starting points towards meeting the statutory expectations of the DfE guidance and providing a curriculum that meets the physical, social, relational and emotional needs of their pupils. Many schools will already be teaching a significant component of the statutory expectations and may simply need to review their curriculum to ensure that they are compliant. That said, to fully meet the needs of all pupils, it is clearly insufficient simply to ensure that the school inspection service (which, in England, is Ofsted – the Office for Standards in Education, Children's Services and Skills) does not criticise them for failing to meet minimal expectations.

Where to begin

There are, of course, a range of commercial resources and support available from organisations such as the PSHE Association (PSHE Association, n.d.) that can help schools plan their curriculum. Additionally, in many local authorities, there remain public health officers who can add expertise and local knowledge. The DfE made it clear that schools should adapt their curriculum to meet local need. Simply put, if your school is near a railway line, please teach more railway safety than if your school is near a canal.

You may be aware of data sources such as ChiMat – the national child and maternal health network – as a source of local health information to inform curriculum planning. Such sources, with anonymous pupil surveys, can also be fed back to pupils. So, if we know that the majority of our students choose not to drink or smoke, or do eat a healthy breakfast, we can use these data to generate positive social norms to influence behaviour. Social Norms Theory (Perkins, 2003) suggests that (young) people do what they do because they assume that everybody else is doing that. Reporting back to a group of school pupils the healthy behaviours that most of them choose (e.g. eating breakfast, or not having sex before the age of 16) reinforces those positive messages and can influence behaviour.

There is also a wealth of tacit information to be gleaned from the police, youth and community workers, and lunch-time assistants, who will know the local community, changes and concerns more intimately than some teaching staff. A major source of intelligence about the needs of our pupils are, of course, children and young people themselves. It is always time well spent for the PSHE lead to have a cup of tea and a biscuit with pupils, not just with higher attainers, but also with children in receipt of free school meals, reluctant attenders and marginalised groups, to discuss the school's current provision, or possibly 'What might a cousin of yours, starting at our school, need?'

Armed with an understanding of why and how the statutory components of PSHE should be implemented, schools then need to consult with parents and carers to establish policy. Although this is a statutory requirement, it is good practice to regularly review policy and pedagogy and involve representatives from the whole school community. 'Consultation' does not allow parental veto of the curriculum, but should ensure that provision is appropriately adapted to respond to local sensitivities.

How do we teach PSHE?

In a knowledge-rich curriculum, teachers can easily become 'fillers of empty vessels'. There are proven approaches regarding column addition or quadratic equations, phonics and Shakespearean quotes. Telling young people what to do, based on what we did (or didn't do) twenty or more years ago, without the internet in your back pocket, is unlikely to be relevant. Research (Ofsted, 2013) suggests that interactive, participatory styles of learning, such as discussion, role-play, conscience corridor, or presenting to their classmates, are far more likely to enable young people to develop the knowledge, skills, attributes and ultimately the behaviours that we would wish for them to adopt.

This has impact on pedagogy but also the paramount importance of creating a safe and appropriate learning environment, where potentially sensitive issues can be discussed, and values explored. This is highly skilled work, which can be learned but should not be left to the vagaries of chance or simply to a colleague who is a few lessons light on their timetable. Establishing and maintaining a safe and appropriate learning environment with a group agreement, co-constructed with pupils to encourage 'ownership', such as 'no personal questions' to prevent personal disclosure and 'treat others with respect' in advance of any potentially sensitive discussions is incredibly important, not just to young people's learning, but to their reputation, dignity and wellbeing. The same is true for teachers faced with questions like 'Have you ever been drunk?' or 'What does sex feel like?'. Here, the ground rules can be invoked (e.g. 'I'm not going to answer that from a personal point of view but I have heard some people say …'), which also model distancing techniques such as 'somebody I know'. These are really effective to encourage safe discussion and allow pupils to discuss sensitive issues without personal disclosure. It is equally essential that we have our responses prepared, if only to allow us to gently but firmly keep our personal life private, or simply to have rehearsed 'That's a great question, but you're going to have to give me a minute or two to think about the best way to answer that' to model the importance of considered reflection. This has significant implications for ongoing, high-quality continuing professional development (CPD).

Going further than statutory guidance

The statutory expectations, although welcomed, are limited and neglect to mention the importance of teaching and learning about essential aspects of life, such as personal finance, loss and bereavement. Personal finance, of course, makes a major contribution to physical health, emotional wellbeing and harmonious family and personal relationships. Managing the loss of a relationship or a loved one was always hugely important, even before Covid claimed lives; holidays, rites of adolescent passage and family celebrations are also important learning topics that contribute to wellbeing. Schools must ensure that these issues are taught to enable children and young people to improve attainment but also to stay safe, healthy and happy, potentially for the rest of their lives.

This briefest of skims cannot do justice to a sensitive and sophisticated curriculum area which deals with the most profound human emotions and experiences. When we get it right, teaching and learning within PSHE, with its contribution to behaviour, attitudes and personal development, makes a significant contribution to the culture and ethos of the school. This, in turn, impacts on attendance and punctuality, disruption and engagement with learning, and so can have a powerful effect on attainment. Happy, healthy children learn better and are more likely to have a significant impact on staff retention, recruitment, workload and wellbeing. What's not to like?

I remain in awe of the phenomenal professional response of educators everywhere to the pandemic. Now may not be the best time to introduce additional curriculum demands, but there are a number of win-wins, not just to meet statutory or inspection expectations, but to enable children and young people to keep themselves safe and healthy and enhance the wellbeing of the adults who love and care for them.

If you are involved in education, you can positively contribute to the statutory components of PSHE. This is not just an immediate imperative but could help to enhance education and outcomes for a generation.

Over to you

The questions below may guide you in exploring how your school might drive pupil engagement and attainment through PSHE:

- What local, regional or national drivers are there to support PSHE in your school?
- What are the health needs of your pupils, and what data can you call upon to evidence these?
- What are you already doing that works, and how much can you build on this?
- What are the CPD needs of your staff?
- What more evidence/resources do you need to support you to transform the learning and life chances of your pupils?

References

Department of Health (2012) *Annual Report of the Chief Medical Officer 2012. Our Children Deserve Better: Prevention Pays.* London. Available online at: https://assets.publishing.service.gov.uk/government/uploads/system/uploads/attachment_data/file/255237/2901304_CMO_complete_low_res_accessible.pdf (Accessed 25 February 2021).

DfE (2019) *Relationships Education, Relationships and Sex Education (RSE) and Health Education.* Available online at: https://consult.education.gov.uk/pshe/relationships-education-rse-health-education/supporting_documents/20170718_Draft guidance for consultation.pdf (Accessed 25 February 2021).

DfE (2020) *Guidance: Personal, social, health and economic (PSHE) education.* Available online at: www.gov.uk/government/publications/personal-social-health-and-economic-education-pshe/personal-social-health-and-economic-pshe-education#personal-social-health-and-economic-education (Accessed 3 March 2021).

Ofsted (2013) Not yet good enough: personal, social, health and economic education in schools. Available online at: www.gov.uk/government/publications/not-yet-good-enough-personal-social-health-and-economic-education (Accessed 25 February 2021).

Perkins, H.W. (2003). *The Social Norms Approach to Preventing School and College Age Substance Abuse: A Handbook for Educators, Counselors, and Clinicians.* San Francisco, CA: Jossey-Bass.

PSHE Association (n.d.) Available online at: www.pshe-association.org.uk/ (Accessed 25 February 2021).

PSHE Education Strategic Partners Group Members (2018) Statutory PSHE Education. Available online at: www.pshe-association.org.uk/system/files/PSHE workload report FINAL version 4 6 2018.pdf (Accessed 25 February 2021).

Public Health England (2014) The link between pupil health and wellbeing and attainment. Available online at: https://assets.publishing.service.gov.uk/government/uploads/system/uploads/attachment_data/file/370686/HT_briefing_layoutvFINALvii.pdf (Accessed 25 February 2021).

Teenage Pregnancy Independent Advisory Group (TPIAG) (2010) Teenage pregnancy: Past successes – future challenges. Available online at: www.gov.uk/government/publications/teenage-pregnancy-past-successes-future-challenges (Accessed 25 February 2021).

SECTION FIVE
INCLUDE WELL

24

A MAN IN A WOMAN'S WORLD

Collated by Kimberley Evans, with sections by Matthew Brooker and Chris Reddy

When I was writing my contributions for this book, I began thinking that many of the strategies suggested were very much aimed at women, but then I questioned myself: were they? Or was I being really stereotypical in thinking that many men don't regularly meditate or use essential oils? This led to a rabbit warren of thoughts; when people talk about wellbeing, do men and women think of different things? Do men push back from what are seen as the traditional ways of wellbeing? Or are they doing plenty of things for their wellbeing but in different ways? What boosts one person's wellbeing can be the thing that depletes another's.

I decided to investigate and get a group of men together to tell me their thoughts. There was a mix of primary and secondary, teaching and leadership, ages and cultures.

Initially, what came through was a difference in the terminology for wellbeing within schools. Some were very much focused on workload. The thinking that wellbeing in schools is reducing workload so you are less stressed and have more time to do what you like to do. A gentle push further brought up the issue that wellbeing is probably seen as performance-focused with men. As I delved deeper, we started to discuss wellbeing on a more personal level and the experiences they'd had showed that wellbeing is a lot harder to work on as a man. Especially a man in a woman's world.

They were very comfortable with taking responsibility on some levels, engaging with exercise and healthy eating. These things can be so varied that they are easily accessible to men. The same as doing something for their own enjoyment. Many spoke about hobbies and pastimes; they may not be the same ideas as what many women do – e.g. gaming, drinking with mates, sending each other rude memes – but it makes them happy and that is a vital cog in wellbeing. It's important to remember that we can't put wellbeing in a box and say that is the only way it works; it is different for every individual. It is not yoga, or cake, or watching a boxing match for that matter, it is doing more of what lights you up and makes you happy.

But one way that men definitely struggle with wellbeing is the mental health side of things. True, exercise, healthy eating and sleep go hand in hand with mental health, but if they don't have an outlet for their everyday worries as well as their overriding fears and stresses, then those things will only have so much effect. If you are a woman reading this, you might be rolling your eyes right now, thinking, 'stress, they don't know stress – try being a mum and a teacher, then you'll know what stress is,' but please read this with an open mind and really think about the men in your setting and how they might be feeling.

> 'Women don't know how to react when a man opens up.'

One man spoke of a time that he opened up in the staffroom about having a bad day, nothing huge, just a usual bad day, the type that women in the staffroom talk about every day. But it was taken completely out of context and everyone thought there was something seriously wrong, that he wasn't coping and needed help. He was simply trying to chat about his day in the way women do all the time.

> 'If a man says they are having a bad day, people think it is catastrophic and everyone panics.'

> 'Women have natural networks and friendships within schools. It is easy for them to make connections and a support network. It's harder for men. If we get together with women in a room then people talk, if I need a shoulder to cry on or a hug then it is frowned upon.'

Again, this is a consequence of the gender split, but it's also our societal preconceptions. The British culture of having a 'stiff upper lip' doesn't help, but it is also us jumping to conclusions and assuming things that blatantly aren't true.

> 'If we say we're not coping or even that we just need help in some way, we are seen as being soft or even looking for excuses.'

'Men need to have a voice' was met with many nods of the collective heads. Further discussion led to men needing help with how to deal with everyday stresses as they are expected to just get on with it. We talked about counselling and supervision, but there is also a need for much simpler things, like connections and friendships. The School Workforce Census shows that, in 2019, male teachers made up only 24% of the overall demographic of the education profession (National Statistics, 2019). That is immediately going to make it harder for men to find people to open up to and make connections with within the profession. We discussed solutions for this; message groups that have been set up across Trusts seemed popular, and also ones set up through social media interests. The men in your setting, or you yourself reading this as a man, may know what would work best for your colleagues. Ask them what they need, what would help. There are support groups around; look for @MenTeachPrimary on Twitter, and I run 'Well-being? It's a man thing' once a month. After spending time researching this topic, I know that, on the surface, men seem to be doing ok; not great, but ok. Scratch a little further and you find that many would really appreciate some help in this area. We just need to be brave enough to scratch!

Big boys don't cry

Matthew Brooker

The phrase 'big boys don't cry' has always stuck with me. One of the lowest points in my teaching career came just over five years ago; I had just got married and we were trying to have a baby. I had been appointed as Assistant Headteacher at a school which wasn't in the best of places. It was a mammoth task. I felt overwhelmed on a daily basis, anxious due to violent children and parents, and had terrible nerves about my own teaching performance. I sat in my classroom one Tuesday evening and I just cried, wondering if it would ever get any better.

I'd be a liar if I said that I haven't felt like that since, but that was the point I realised that something had to change. My favourite phrase is, 'you cannot pour from an empty cup'. This is so true. I began to shift my focus to how I can better help myself. What could I do to ensure I do not become this empty vessel? The answer to this is varied and personal to each person who reads these words. I follow simple steps to ensure that my wellbeing is being catered for.

1. Surround yourself with people who allow you to be you. Don't let someone judge you; I have often apologised for my quirks or eccentricities merely to accommodate others. People who allow me to be me are the people I want surrounding me.

2. Physical exercise has benefited me greatly. I jump on my mountain bike and blast a few miles. I play golf twice a month, I commit to a hobby, which pays dividends. It calms me and relaxes me. Finally, my second home – the gym. Releasing endorphins allows me to think more clearly (after this is when I am at my most focused part of the day).

3. Spending time with my family, friends and loved ones. I mean really spending time. Listening and engaging with them, shutting down from 'work talk'. My

family are wonderful at not asking the usual, 'so, how's work going?' Instead, we laugh and talk, to be quite frank, utter nonsense.

4. Spend time in your own happy place. I walk by the sea (we are fortunate to live by the sea). This calms and inspires me. It gives me a different perspective, which quite often is when I am at my most creative.

Ultimately, there is no right or wrong to wellbeing, particularly for men. Many societal changes have meant that men can or can't show their feelings and emotions. However, do not bury down those feelings; take time for yourself. Whether that is through exercise, gaming, a drink with friends, going to the cinema (or bingeing on that Netflix series that everyone talks about), talking to someone about utter nonsense and, dare I say it, having a massage or any other self-care treatment. Wellbeing is not a one size fits all, however it is a what size fits you. Do something once a day that makes you happy, even if it is for five minutes. Just switch off and let something completely immerse you. Through this, your inner happiness can be achieved.

Find your thing

Chris Reddy

For years, physical activity and sport has played a huge part in my life. It's only in recent years, however, that I've really understood the benefits it has brought to my life. I've been active for as long as I can remember. I've taken part in school sport and extracurricular activities since primary school and represented all the schools I attended, for a variety of different sports. Following this, I went on to university to study Physical Education (PE), and later became a PE teacher. Even with ten years of experience as a PE teacher, I still hadn't fully realised how important physical activity was to me and my wellbeing.

In fact, on reflection, it was only really when my wellbeing was truly tested that I realised what physical activity did for my wellbeing. After losing my dad quickly to cancer, whilst at the same time transitioning to a new role in an intense educational environment, I quickly realised that I had a lot to deal with. I was aiming to support my family whilst working seriously long hours to fit it all in. I look back now and wonder how I would have coped if my kids had been around then. No one offered to help. Why would they? I outwardly presented to most that I was doing great.

Two things gave me the strength and the energy to get through this in a positive way. Two things that I now realise are well nurtured and well-oiled habits – exercise and connection. My exercise did not stop, and I had two key people to talk to, and talk to regularly. My wife and a female colleague at work. I look back and wonder: why was it that I opened up to women? Was it because these were people who knew me well, or was it because they were women? I suspect a bit of both. Why is it that I would have found it harder talking about my wellbeing to a man? I've worked hard in my life to foster a close and trusting friendships group, yet I still didn't speak about my struggles to any of my male friends or colleagues at the time.

Wellbeing is counterintuitive. When you're feeling low, the 'tortoise method' is often the most appealing thing to do. Get your head in that shell and hide from the world, it's much safer. Actually, when feeling low, the best thing to do is exercise, talk to others, reach out for help or do more of what you love.

At the time, I really don't remember thinking, 'Ok, I'm a bit low, I need to go and run or talk to someone', it was just something that I did. I look back and know that the habits that I'd fostered as a child in playing, staying active and spending so much time with my friends had come back to serve me through the most challenging time in my life.

When we are busy, stressed and being tested at work, the things that we find fun or joy in are often the things we drop first. Our hobbies and personal interests can be seen as luxuries. However, these are the things we need in our lives and, when we are low, we need to work to keep these front and centre in our mind. These are what rejuvenates us, gets us through difficult times and gives us the creativity and release from daily life that we need. It doesn't need to be exercise or social connection; this is just what works for me.

The @teacher5aday concept works as a daily reminder for me. A reminder that wellbeing is unique to everyone and it's very personal. It helps me support me. It also helps me support my family, my colleagues, my clients, and the young people in my care. You can support your wellbeing by giving, taking notice, learning, exercising or connecting – there is something for everyone.

Socialising and exercising are my non-negotiable hobby habits.

Hobbies matter; find your thing.

References

National Statistics (2019) *School Workforce Census*. Available online at: https://explore-education-statistics.service.gov.uk/find-statistics/school-workforce-in-england (Accessed 5 March 2021).

25

FLYING THE FLAG! HOW TO DEVELOP A SAFE PLACE FOR THE LGBTQ+ COMMUNITY

Alex Purdie

I came out when I was seventeen, so felt pretty confident and comfortable entering the teaching career as a proud gay man. I had a positive coming out story as my family and friends were supportive, so after years of thinking this moment would never come, when it did it was amazing to live as my authentic self. I never had any negative experiences in my teacher training year nor in any schools I worked in, so it was pretty easy to just be me. I think if I couldn't be out, it would have made a massive difference; I wouldn't be able to share stories when my students ask me how my weekend/ holidays have been as I wouldn't be able to mention my partner or when I attend pride events, or to be a role model and so on. Whilst I totally recognize that being gay is a huge part of my life, it's not the biggest part. I refer to myself as a teacher who is gay, not a gay teacher, and for me that's important.

One of my best friends secured her job on the same day as me and there were lots of rumours asking whether we were dating; students would ask us both, and we'd just laugh about it. She never answered the students as she fully respected that it was my choice to tell the kids, but it didn't bother me. So, the next time they asked I responded 'No, I'm not dating Miss XXX, I'm gay'. There was silence, looking around at each other and then they asked, 'have you been to pride?' and that was it – we got talking about sexuality and the LGBTQ+ community. In my opinion, young people are the least judgmental people in society and they just accepted it. I also feel it's important to be out as I have and will continue to teach LGBTQ+ young people and I want them to know they are not invisible in society; they have a voice, an opinion and a right to be themselves, and if me being out helps with this, that's great.

I think it's important to mention to the readers that I completely recognise that, for some, it's not as easy (or necessary) for a multitude of reasons to be out, and possibly they have had negative experiences in schools, too. I have the utmost respect for those people and only hope they feel comfortable to do it one day. At the end of the day, your life is *your* journey, and we should travel through it however we see fit.

I think there are lots of things any workplace can do that would have a positive impact for the LGBTQ+ community. I think there should be an inclusion representative/lead, non-gendered toilets, visible representation in terms of people but also posters/displays. I know many people think this can be tokenistic, but I strongly feel the need for LGBTQ+ themed displays, flags, posters etc. as we all need to remember that the LGBTQ+ community exists. Another powerful practical thing that can be done is ensuring that any type of homo/transphobic behaviour is dealt with correctly and seriously. When leadership/management mirror this inclusive ethos, it's incredibly powerful and will allow LGBTQ+ people to feel safe and comfortable.

I also think the use of allies is extremely positive. In my school (if COVID-19 didn't exist) our aim this year for the LGBTQ+ team was to promote and encourage the use of allies across the school, whether it be staff, students or the local community. We have designed a card which can be displayed in classrooms/offices/public spaces from an image I saw on Facebook; we have allies wearing rainbow lanyards, attending the LGBTQ+ club, but the biggest and most effective way for an ally to show strength is to challenge any offensive behaviour and language. Whenever I speak to colleagues or friends about this, it always reminds me of a Twitter friend @afergusonteach1 and the hashtag #bearebel which asks: how can you 'be a rebel?' I encourage people to have those challenging and difficult conversations, speak out and ask *why* they are using that language. This approach in my opinion is a subtle but brave way to show support and talk about the inequalities that exist across the country … no, the world.

In my own school, I'm lucky enough to have only had positive experiences in the workplace, yet if LGBTQ+ wasn't considered in some initiatives, I have an amazingly supportive senior leadership team (SLT) who would fix it right away. However, I do know of schools that don't include or consider LGBTQ+ due to the fact 'we only have around five gay kids'. Yes, this was actually said in a school. I think that's why I'm very literal about making sure LGBTQ+ is visible in schools, as then no one will forget or consider it as a 'tick box'. We have painted rainbow bricks, the progress pride flag flying outside both buildings, displays promoting strong and proud role models in each building, we celebrate Pride and LGBTQ+ History Month, have dedicated assemblies, a linked Governor, dedicated sessions within our Personal, Social, Health and Economics Education (PSHEE) curriculum, a diversity lead on our student body, a LGBTQ+ staff team, and we encourage our staff and students to talk and ask questions. Whilst some may see this as impressive, the team and I always feel we can do more and won't stop (which probably means we won't for a long time).

When thinking of good systems to put in place in a school to help with feeling part of the school family, just think of PAPSS:

- Policies: Have a strong set of policies (Equality, Diversity and Inclusion), guidelines and protocols that all aspects of the school community are aware of.

- Allies: Encourage people to talk and ask questions and recognise the importance and power our allies have.

- Pride: Ensure all your LGBTQ+ students/staff and their allies are proud of what we do in our school community and most importantly be proud of themselves!

- Support from the top: I feel it's incredibly important to ensure your SLT/Governing body/Management team are aware of how you want to improve inclusion in your school or workplace. We have a passionate linked Governor (also an ally) who is a huge champion; we also have an SLT who are proud of the work we all do in our school to make it as inclusive as possible.

- Speak: It's so important to speak, whether that is asking questions, challenging behaviour, contacting parents and outside agencies. Speaking is key to moving forward and ensuring our community becomes inclusive, safe, accepting and kind to all.

26

WELLBEING IN A CULTURALLY DIVERSE SOCIETY

Collated by Kimberley Evans

When we are all living in such a culturally diverse society, we need to make sure our whole school wellbeing offer is actually meeting the needs of everyone. Different cultures, religions and beliefs all have different needs for wellbeing and these are often overlooked in the drive to have cohesion and unity.

I could write an entire book on this subject alone, so I'll start by saying this is most definitely the tip of the iceberg, and please don't be offended if an important point is missed. I have tried to pull together some experiences and viewpoints that will make you think about the pupils and staff in your setting and how you can accommodate their particular diverse wellbeing needs within your community.

Religious festivals and cultural traditions

Respecting and celebrating different religious festivals needs to go further than covering them in lessons and assemblies. It is more than putting some displays up at Holi or having cultural food on the canteen menu. It means giving proper consideration to staff and pupils' beliefs and how they will impact the school year. Knowing when Ramadan falls each year can really help pupils during exams, in case the exam boards need to be informed. Avoiding late evening meetings or parents' evenings for staff during the time of Ramadan could have a hugely positive impact on staff wellbeing. Make connections with your staff and pupils and really get to know what is important to them, their religions and cultures.

As a secular, and semi-practising Jew, there are certain festivals that are extremely important to me. These include the most solemn and important day in our calendar, Yom Kippur (The Day of Atonement) and Rosh Hashana (Jewish New Year). These holy days generally fall in September or October, right at the start of the academic year, and when starting the year with a new class it has always been difficult to take the days off to attend synagogue with family. Despite this, I have always been lucky in that my headteachers have allowed me the time off for these festivals. I am aware that other practising Jews have been less fortunate, and some have had to take their cases up with Local Authorities. I would have found this extremely challenging for my own wellbeing, as religion and family are so closely linked, especially in Judaism.

Yom Kippur is a fast day, where we fast for 25 hours from dusk to dusk. We are also not permitted to carry out any work on this day. I know fasting whilst working would be extremely challenging, and I know some other faiths have fast days on which they are permitted to work. In my experience schools I have worked in have been supportive of staff and pupils who are required to fast whilst at school, for example allowing students and staff to be excused from PE lessons. This positive attitude to diversity has a strong impact on the wellbeing not only of the staff directly affected, but also of other staff and in particular those from other minority groups, such as me!

Karen Connolly

Appearance and uniform rules

From discussion with students and parents, hair is so important for identity for any student. And for their wellbeing it is important we ensure our policies are fair and inclusive.

Uniform and rules around appearance can be a contentious issue. Do strict rules help or hinder the wellbeing of students? Does the colour of their hair or the length of their socks really make that much difference to their learning? In some communities it does make a difference, giving students a sense of unity and family. It can also help to prevent bullying. But strict rules can also strip away their identity.

The original hair policy at our school stated no 'multiple' braids. This was removed many years ago and rightly so. Largely because the profile of the school began to change to have more BAME students (and a change of leadership).

As with all policies, we look to review. The current policy is hair that is streaked or dyed is 'not permitted.' But lots of girls have lovely balayages/ombres that we do not challenge.

However, if you wear braids as many girls with Afro hair do, if they want contrasting colours it looks very stark, even if it's natural colours, as they are separate braids and maybe do not 'merge' as well – so leaves them more open to it being challenged.

We do not allow shaved hair below a grade 3, but many boys with Afro hair like to keep it short for ease of maintenance. So we will be revising the wording to make it more inclusive and more at the discretion of the school.

Coaching/counselling

Some schools/academy trusts offer counselling or therapy sessions. Which already is great – but personally I'm never inclined to it because I know off the bat I will be spending more time explaining my background and religion for context purposes, than actually benefiting from the counselling.

Offering help such as coaching and supervision is a huge step in the right direction in terms of staff wellbeing, and please don't feel that voices like this are throwing a helping hand back in your face. But if it is going to work for the individual, it has to be the right fit for them. It might be easier to employ one coach to do sessions for all the staff, but that is a complete waste of money if that coach is not the right fit for everyone. What is much more cost and value effective is to match people correctly. Spend time searching for a diverse pool of people your staff can sign up to. That will then avoid situations like this:

I did have some coaching but held back with certain experiences and discussions just because I felt like I had to explain myself and it wasn't worth the 'hassle' so to speak.

Trainee teachers/new staff

It's making sure we are telling our trainee teachers what their pupils from different backgrounds to their own might experience. In the context I work in, most students are white and their schools are massively majority white so we try to give them a sense of what they need to consider to support those from BAME backgrounds and also how being inclusive in their practice is central to supporting wellbeing in their students – making them feel part of the community and considered and seen. We encourage them to develop their knowledge and show them how to work towards them being allies for BAME colleagues and pupils.

Dr Anjali Shah, Senior Lecturer in Education, University of Chester

This can also apply to staff moving to new areas or communities. It could become part of the induction process to make new staff fully aware of the diversities of your school community and how their needs are different. It's a simple thing that is very often forgotten.

BAME/Global Majority

'There was always the pressure to always be the finished article already,'

said Shabnam Anam. She was a headteacher and felt the extreme pressures placed on her, by herself and others.

> I would feel compared to all the time, and imposter syndrome was always there. But we (people in the Global Majority) always feel we just need to deal with it, get on with it. Otherwise others would say 'see, told you so'.

We talked about her South Asian heritage and how, from a very early age, she felt the pressures.

> There is always going to be a disadvantage, that will be there until we are on the same starting line-up as white people, so parents instill in us a work ethic that is highly pressured.

She went on to discuss how she finally broke free of this, and her joy of seeing her mum accept that it wasn't a healthy attitude to have, even though it is deep-rooted in culture.

> There are many cultural reasons why we are not kinder to ourselves.

I asked if she thought this was still the case now; with the generations of children coming through the education system, are these cultural pressures just as high?

> Families from the Global Majority will always feel that their children need to have a head start. There are constant barriers and they need an advantage, any advantage. In that way race can actually be a safeguarding issue.

I asked Shabnam what she thought could be done, going forward. We discussed the difference between race, religion and culture. A lot is being done about being more understanding about race and religion, but cultures need more. Cultures can be the family, the household, and that is far more individual than general race and religion.

> Schools need to understand the deep culture of their students and staff and how they differ so greatly. They need to really get to know them and how they work. They need to see the individuals.

27

DISABILITY WELLBEING – WHY INCLUSION MATTERS FOR DISABLED CHILDREN

Elizabeth Wright

In the beginning, my parents were my biggest advocates. I certainly wasn't aware of this. As a child, I was happy, safe, and enjoyed playing with my toys and the new family puppy. I was not aware of anything untoward about my lived experience, anything that should give me concern. Only, there was something about my life that concerned my parents, something that was concerning doctors, occupational therapists, family members, neighbours and so on.

Born with a range of impairments that collectively are medically called 'congenital limb deficiency', I was living my best childhood with missing limbs. Half my right arm is missing, I'm missing bones in my left forearm and hand, which resulted in a missing finger and my thumb and another finger being joined together. And half my right leg is missing, meaning I wear a prosthetic leg to walk.

This is my normal. Always has been and always will be. And as a child, I never recognised that my normal was already impacting my lived experience and opportunities to thrive. My parents recognised the impact though; they were fiercely aware of it, and it is why they fought so hard to get me into mainstream schooling, even though, in the early eighties, a disabled child in a mainstream school was very rarely done.

I remember, as a three-year-old, sitting on top of the canteen counter at the local primary school, watching the canteen ladies – my mum included – whizzing back and forth, packing orders. A cheese sandwich for that child, a packet of chicken-flavoured crisps for that one and, typically Australian, a couple of Cadbury Koala chocolates in that packet. Children would be hammering at the canteen windows, their voices echoing around the brick shelter. Eager for their food, they barely noticed the little girl with a missing arm and prosthetic leg, gazing at them in awe from inside the window she was positioned at.

Mum was smart. As a newly-badged advocate for disabled people, courtesy of me, mum figured the best way to fight the system was to make friends inside it. By bringing me to the canteen with her, she ensured the teachers and other staff got to know me. They got to know about my impairment, they got to know about what I could and couldn't do, they became as comfortable around me as I was becoming around them. Just before I was due to be enrolled at my local primary school, mum had a final tussle with the New South Wales (NSW) Education Department – which she kind of won. My initial experience of primary school would be on a three-month trial. If I, or the school, failed this trial, I would be promptly sent to the special needs school in the next suburb.

Mum knew we wouldn't fail.

After three months, the Education Department agreed to let me stay on at the school and I flourished. Because I had been at the school from the get-go, my peers saw me as one of them. In fact, I experienced positive discrimination a lot; I had one friend who wanted to do my homework for me all the time (I was too much of a goody-two-shoes to take her up on the offer).

On reflection, I can see that there was an unfair advantage to my fellow pupils on my being included with them – they got to see positive disability representation through me. They got to see that a disabled child wasn't defined by their impairment, that a disabled child was just like them in many ways. I didn't have positive disability representation. Being the only pupil with a disability meant that I had no one who really understood my lived experience. They didn't understand how frustrating stairs were for me – often my friends would disappear up or down the stairs and have to wait for me as I laboriously went one step at a time. They didn't understand why I got angry with them at playtime when they would want to do an activity that excluded me. That's not to say that they didn't always try to include me in stuff, so much so that they did end up teaching me how to skip rope and play handball. Expressing one's feelings about feeling excluded is difficult; and then there was the unintentional bullying. When it came to positing different identities on ourselves through play, I was never the princess or the heroine, I was called 'E.T.' or 'Jake the Peg' (a pirate character created by disgraced Australian entertainer Rolf Harris).

There was also no representation in the staff. As far as I knew, no staff member, in any of my schools, had a disability. Or no physical disability. There were no adults that I could look up to and go 'Ah, there is my potential, there is a career I could have'. I also had to contend with some teachers whose attitudes toward disability left a lot to be desired. Sometimes, differentiation for disabled pupils is needed, but misapplied it can do more harm than good.

Mrs K was my Year 3 craft teacher. We had her every Tuesday and I liked her and she liked me. Generally supportive, she had always let me take part in crafts, never questioning my ability to cut with scissors or colour-in with pencils or paint with thick goopy acrylics. But one week we were to start weaving. A more complex activity, but one that I knew I could do. I was so excited to give it a go. Sitting down for craft class that afternoon, I watched as Mrs K put weaving looms and yarn down on everyone's table, except mine. On mine, she put down some colouring-in pictures and pencils.

I couldn't understand why she had done this. I tried to explain that I wanted to try the weaving, but she wouldn't listen to me. I went home in tears. This went on for a couple of Tuesdays and, in the end, my mum had to visit the school and talk to the teacher and the principal. Next time I had craft class, Mrs K put a loom and yarn down on my table, without so much as a smile or look of apology.

Disability representation, in education, matters. It mattered then, it matters now, and whilst disabled children are being included in mainstream schooling more and more, there is still a lack of representation in teaching staff, in the curriculum, and in the media that children are exposed to on a daily basis. How do we change this? By addressing our unconscious biases around disability, tackling our teacher recruitment processes, ensuring that our curricula are representative of disability, and establishing accessibility as a core aspect of universal design, especially in school buildings. Why should we address representation? Because lack of representation feeds an ableist society that will continuously hold disabled children and adults back from achieving their potential.

Ableism is deep-seated in our communities. Insidious, it weaves its judgement and assumptions through all facets of life. It impacts disabled children from the very beginning of their lives, and most notably during their education. It is during these formative years that disabled children develop an internalised ableism that impacts their very confidence and self-esteem. Ableism, quite literally, impacts a disabled child's wellbeing every single day – even if they don't realise this is happening.

What is ableism? Ableism sits snuggly amongst racism, sexism, homophobia, ageism and so on. It is discrimination towards an individual based on their impairment or condition. It can be expressed in a multitude of ways: through physical inaccessibility to a space, through stereotypes and tropes that influence beliefs about disability, exclusion through attitudes and beliefs towards disabled people, through ignorance, through misunderstanding, through bullying and harassment, through hate and fear. And it starts young.

I noted earlier that I had friends at school; in fact, I only ever remember having one explicit experience of bullying, and some of my boy friends put that to rest very quickly on my behalf. And yet, these same boys who I called friends, when it came to the very cringe-worthy Australian primary school activity of summer, 'barn dancing', never wanted to hold my hand. They never wanted to touch me. And that stung. It made me feel self-conscious. It made me feel other-ed. It didn't help that I developed crushes on some of these boy friends – John, Michael and Sam. Whilst other girl friends were coupling up (yes, those pre-teen hormones were kicking in), I was left on the outside of this experience of growing up, so desperately wishing I had an in.

What needs to be recognised and normalised and dismantled swiftly from our society is this application of othering. We need to address the segregation of people that still happens based on that group or individual's identity characteristics. And whilst there are many steps forward in dismantling discrimination, exclusion and oppression, as I have illustrated, at least anecdotally, it is often the smaller slights, the throw-away lines, or subtle behaviours that can accumulate into a devastating impact on one's self-esteem, wellbeing and confidence.

When I was in my 20s, I started my Fine Art degree and discovered disability theory and politics. What I was reading felt revolutionary. It was revolutionary. Growing up in a world that was not made for disabled people, I had always believed that the discrimination, exclusion and repugnance expressed towards me as a child had been my fault. That my body was not made for this world and therefore I had to try and change myself to fit more. Since my teens I had attempted this by 'passing'. Passing is a term used in the disability community that describes attempting to appear as non-disabled as possible. In the middle of an Australian summer, on school 'no uniform' days, I would wear thick jeans to hide my prosthetic leg and cardigans or jackets to hide my arm. I made myself both physically and emotionally uncomfortable for the comfort of my non-disabled peers and teachers.

Exploring disability theory and politics, I came across a theory that astounded me and made sense to me. The Social Model of Disability (Oliver, 2013) identifies systemic barriers, such as negative attitudes and exclusion, inaccessibility, and under-representation, as being the inherent cause of disability; not the impairment or condition that an individual has. Developed by UK disability academic Mike Oliver, the social model acknowledges the medical needs of a disabled individual, but clearly shows that exclusion and discrimination stems from a world that rejects impairment and illness. Quite simply, disabled children and adults live in a world that has not been created with their needs, wants and desires in mind.

The social model tells us that if we make changes, both big and small, to our environment, to our beliefs, to representation, we can diminish the discrimination that disabled people experience. This includes education settings. I imagine what my life as a disabled child may have been like if the social model of disability had been firmly in place in my community.

I imagine that, at my birth, the doctors would have congratulated my parents on the birth of their very unique little girl. I imagine that our neighbours, family friends, and strangers would've exclaimed what a beautiful baby I was, instead of asking when my parents were going to put me in a home for disabled people. I imagine that the NSW Education Department wouldn't have quibbled at all in allowing me to attend my mainstream primary school. I imagine that all of my teachers would've encouraged me to try new things and trusted my own judgement about my abilities. I imagine that the boys in my years would've grabbed my hand without fear as they swung me through the barn dances. I imagine that I would've felt like I belonged in this world, from the very beginning of my life; that I would've been embraced for my differences and not set apart.

Perhaps, this is what we need to aim for now with our disabled children, creating a world where their needs, wants, and desires are met; where their wellbeing and self-esteem is built up. Where their potential is recognised and achieved. And so, I challenge you to identify examples of ableism in your own spaces, your own school, your own community, and consider how this might be impacting the self-esteem and wellbeing of disabled people in your life. What can you do to change this ableism and become a disability ally?

References

Oliver, M. (2013) 'The social model of disability: thirty years on', *Disability & Society*, 28(7): 1024–1026.

28

LANGUAGE AND STIGMA AROUND MENTAL HEALTH

Jen Beer

What?

Throughout this book, there have been many opportunities to reflect on the importance of mental health and wellbeing. Just through picking up this book, you have demonstrated a passion for creating an environment in which children and the whole school community can thrive. There are, however, a number of barriers you may face when trying to make changes, not least because mental health remains a term which means different things to different people; and mental health stigma, although slowly shifting, still remains.

This chapter will explore some ways in which we can tackle mental health stigma and why it is so important that we do so, as well as shining a light on the important role that language has to play in being an instrument for change.

There are many different words used to describe mental health – wellbeing, emotional or mental wellbeing, wellness, resilience, happiness. It is always useful in a school (or any environment) to develop a shared language, including parents and carers wherever possible, as this will form the basis for enabling important conversations about mental health. Mental health literacy is defined as understanding how to achieve and keep good mental health; understanding mental ill health and its treatments and reducing the stigma associated with it; and improving our competencies around managing and caring for our own mental health, when to seek help and where from (Kutcher et al., 2016).

Developing mental health literacy within your school or college will help children to be able to understand and express how they are feeling more effectively, as well as helping them to become more considerate and empathetic adults.

There still remains a stigma in relation to talking about how we feel, particularly in telling people that we are struggling to cope, or in asking for help. This is why it is so important that we create school environments in which everybody possesses the language to meaningfully talk about mental health. Mental health stigma can be more pronounced for some people than others, depending on their gender, age, experience or culture, and it's important to note that in some cultures mental health is still very much considered a taboo subject, meaning the school can play an incalculably important role in providing a safe space for children to explore this topic and build more positive attitudes towards mental health. We simply cannot afford to ignore stigma or pretend it doesn't exist, as it can prevent a child or young person from a) asking for help, and b) feeling like they 'fit in' or are 'normal'. Such feelings are incredibly isolating for a child or young person experiencing them and, unless tackled early, the negative impacts can continue into adulthood, affecting almost every aspect of their life.

The school environment provides us with a real opportunity to tackle mental health stigma head on, and provides a safe space for children to learn the tools for looking after their mental health and the knowledge of how, when and where to seek help, should they need it.

Why?

Although progress has been made in bringing mental health to the forefront, it is still the case that most of the time when people hear the words 'mental health', they immediately think of 'mental illness'. This can make conversations about mental health feel abstract or irrelevant for everyone who has not (or believes they have not) experienced mental ill health.

Building a shared language around the central concept of mental health being something that we all have serves an important purpose; everyone becomes included and engaged in the topic and it becomes easier to have meaningful conversations about how we can look after and protect our mental health, and how we can support those around us.

We all have a head, so we all have mental health, and for each person, mental health will fluctuate; sometimes we will feel good, sometimes bad, sometimes just OK. The key message then is that it's OK to not be OK, and it's unhelpful to strive to feel constantly good. Once we accept this, we tend to be a lot less hard on ourselves, and potentially others.

However, accepting that our mental health will change over time doesn't mean accepting it as something we have no control over. Just like our physical health, which we can help to protect by eating healthily, being active and seeking help when things go wrong, there are also (often quite similar) things we can do to look after our mental health. Once we accept that, it can be quite empowering.

These things will lower our chances of becoming mentally ill, but they certainly don't remove the risk entirely, and it's important to remind children and young people you work with that developing a mental illness can happen to anyone, sometimes in response to something in their lives, but often seemingly not in response to anything – again, much like physical illness, there doesn't always have to be an obvious cause.

In terms of looking after and protecting our mental health, it is widely accepted that talking about how you feel, and asking for help when you need it, are important ways to improve wellbeing. This is where mental health stigma comes into play and can be a significant barrier for children and young people. It is important that the stigma surrounding mental health is reduced to a point where if someone is struggling, it feels like a natural, or at least 'doable' step to talk to someone and ask for help.

How?

This will be very specific to your particular school community and the people it serves. It is also a huge topic of its own that is very difficult to summarise in a short chapter. But by building a shared language and understanding of mental health, we can progress to making a real difference in people's lives.

Here are a range of relatively simple ways to begin to build a shared language and understanding of mental health within your school, college or other environment for you to start thinking about how to make a positive change.

Start with you

It is helpful, before you do anything else, to take the time to reflect on what mental health means to you. Ask yourself the following questions:

1. What does 'mental health' mean to me – how would I define it?

2. What has been my experience of mental health/mental illness (consider own experiences as well as those of people around you)? How might these experiences have influenced my personal view of mental health?

3. What things help me to improve my own mental health? And what barriers are there to doing these things?

It is important to take this time for reflection for two reasons. Firstly, it can serve as a reminder that we need to look after our own mental health before we can meaningfully support others. Secondly, it can help us to be empathetic and understanding of people's different attitudes towards mental health, and cognisant of any triggers or prejudices that we may have ourselves developed throughout our lives.

Surveys and School Councils

Running surveys and group discussions to gain a better understanding of the differences in how pupils (and teaching staff) think about and understand mental health will help you to work out what you need to do to develop a shared language. You can ask questions like:

1. 'When talking about your feelings or emotions, which of the following words do you use? Mental health – Mood – Emotional Wellbeing – Wellbeing – Happiness – Resilience – Other'.

2. 'Would you ask for help if you were struggling to cope?'

3. 'Who would you go to first if you felt you needed support?'

It can also be useful to gauge and monitor mental health stigma through asking to what extent pupils and/or teachers agree or disagree with the following statements:

'People should just pull themselves together'

'It's OK for people to talk about their mental health'

The responses to all of these questions will show you whether there are significant differences in perceptions and understanding of mental health from children or staff of different genders, ages or cultures.

School vision

Once you have a better understanding of how pupils and staff currently view mental health, it is important to develop a shared school vision, ideally in collaboration with pupils and parents. This vision can be clearly displayed within the school and with the whole school community, and will underpin your whole school approach to mental health.

Lessons

Lessons and short form time activities can be a good way to develop mental health literacy, broaden your pupils' understanding of the topic, and to start to normalise talking about mental health. A quiz focussed on myth-busting can be a useful way to start to build knowledge and understanding, and national mental health charities also host a number of online videos that you could watch to stimulate group discussion.

An example of a short activity that can be used to explore the topic of mental health, is to ask pupils to spend five–ten minutes completing Table 28.1.

Usually people find it easier to complete the second column than the first, and this can provide a useful basis for a conversation about why negative terminology is still often used, what impact the negative words may have on someone, and what terminology we think is most helpful when talking about mental health.

Table 28.1   Mental Health Language Template: The words we use

Positive words we use when talking about mental health	Negative words we use when talking about mental health

Provide opportunities for all young people to share feedback and worries

In order to foster an ethos of talking about mental health and asking for support, there are a number of things you could do. Nurture groups and counselling sessions within the school can be a more formal way to provide opportunities for talking, but there are also a number of smaller things that can help. Confidential worry boxes could be placed around the school – these can either be anonymous or an opportunity to ask for help without having to start a conversation.

Buddy benches in playgrounds have also been a very effective way, particularly in primary schools, to ensure that if a child is feeling lonely or just wants to talk to someone, their friends or peers can support them. Find out more about these, and Playground Wellbeing Buddies, in Thérèse Hoyle's chapter (22).

Finally, make sure that, at regular intervals throughout the year, clear information on how children can access support (in and outside of school) is prominently displayed and communicated verbally.

Challenging stigma

Once you have developed and displayed a clear school vision around mental health and wellbeing, and ensured there are a range of opportunities within the school for a child or young person to talk to someone, it is important to ensure that children feel able to access this support, should they need to. This can be achieved by challenging mental health stigma, normalising conversations about mental health, and modelling positive coping strategies.

Role modelling behaviours

Telling young people what they should do to look after their mental health will not be enough to make a meaningful change; we also need to show them. It can be natural to think that by keeping our insecurities, worries and bad days to ourselves, we are in some way protecting our pupils, but actually by sometimes talking about these things and showing the positive things we ourselves do to cope with everyday challenges, this will show pupils that it's OK for emotions to fluctuate, and that there are things we can all do that can help us to cope. Where possible, it is also useful to encourage parents to take this same approach.

Draw on external role models

In recent years, more and more people have been speaking out about their experience of mental illness, in order to help shift the stigma. Sharing examples of high profile people who have experienced mental illness, and showing that this has not defined their lives or prevented them from achieving incredible things, can be a good way to get a conversation started. It can also be useful to use 'closer to home' examples. For example, you could contact local mental health charities or services to see if they have any young role models willing to share their stories of recovery, coping, and hope.

It's really important to ensure role models that you identify are relatable for your students, by including people from a range of backgrounds, ethnicities, genders, sexualities and ages.

Manage expectations

While enormous progress has been made, mental health stigma still exists and probably will continue to do so for some time. Not everyone knows how best to respond when someone talks to them about how they are feeling. I therefore always tell young people I work with that if you open up to someone about how you're feeling and you don't get the reaction you need, then it's important (although not easy) not to take this personally – it is never possible to know what challenges another person is currently experiencing, or to control their reaction to us. If you don't feel that someone has been able to help you or understood what you have said, then it's important to speak to someone else.

Over to you

Please think about what steps you need to take to develop a shared mental health language and vision within your school or other education setting. Be as specific as you can, adding in timescales and who you may need to help you to achieve each stage of your plan.

- What do you want to achieve? Write down a few sentences to summarise your overall vision for building a shared language and reducing stigma in relation to mental health within your school community.

- What steps do you need to take to achieve your vision? What are the timescales for these steps?

- What barriers might you face, and how will you address these?

- Who else do you need to involve?

  o   Within your school community

  o   Outside of your school community.

References

Kutcher, S., Wei, Y. and Coniglio, C. (2016) 'Mental health literacy: Past, present and future'. *The Canadian Journal of Psychiatry*, 61(3): 154–158.

29

THE EDUCATION SYSTEM AND ME

Holly Evans

The education system and me, we just don't get along. I am Autistic and have ADHD as well as sensory and auditory processing disorders. I am 17 years old and in Year 13, currently studying English, history, anthropology, biology, maths and German for my International Baccalaureate (IB or IBACC) at a grammar school.

In 2020, when the pandemic hit, my GCSEs were cancelled and I was given predicted grades by my teachers. I was finding studying hard then, as I was off my ADHD medication, but I was trying hard to make improvements. I didn't get the chance to improve my work any more than I had already done, as the grades were based on my past work. My post-16 choices were limited due to this and the fact that schools were prioritising their own students. I wanted to move schools as the syllabus was more interesting to me but couldn't get into where I wanted to go. I also needed to think about whether moving to another school was a good idea when at least the teachers at my current school knew me and what I struggle with already. Was it worth starting from scratch? I didn't really have the luxury of doing what my friends were doing and going to another school, as it really was just too much.

But the problems I face in school on a daily basis aren't to do with the pandemic. They have been made much worse by the situation, but they have always been there. They will be there for thousands of other pupils in every single school.

I feel different in school in many ways. I can't write essays (very needed at IB level). I can't take notes when someone is speaking (not just writing down what that person is speaking about but if anyone is speaking I can't concentrate enough to write things down), I struggle to formulate ideas into paragraphs and I feel like I can't understand unless I know everything about that topic. If I ask why, or for more information about things, a teacher will often respond with 'you don't need to know that', but I do. I need to know how things fit into the bigger picture for me to really understand. And I feel like I can't do things (in life in general as well as my school work) unless I truly understand. I need context.

This is intensified by being the only person with autism and ADHD in my year. I feel like the minority because I am the minority. But should that stop me from learning?

'Well learn, then', is a phrase I hear a lot. Often I will say, 'I can't do that', and for adults in my life to reply with 'well learn, then' is not in the slightest bit helpful. If I say 'I don't understand', it is often met with 'Yes, you do!'. How is that helping me to learn? How do you know I know? Are you in my brain? They can be absolutely adamant I can do something. Maybe this is them trying to encourage me, but it doesn't work. All it does is annoy me further. Do teachers know how to teach someone with a neuro-diverse brain? Do they get any training on how our brains think differently? Do they understand how it feels to be so different in our everyday lives?

I don't think they do. And this affects not just my learning but my mental health as well. Imagine feeling misunderstood, left out, not catered for. Every single day of your life.

It's got to the point where I have no interest in listening to a neurotypical person trying to help me, as they don't understand how. They just make it worse.

The school system is built for neurotypicals. The curriculum is written by neuro-typicals. The way we have to work, like writing essays, having tests and exams, doing speaking assessments, is all based on a neurotypical brain. All devised by neurotypi-cals. Yet 20% of the population is neurodiverse. This number could be even higher in schools as the process of diagnosis gets easier. We might get extra time in exams and assessments, but that in itself doesn't help. If I don't understand the question because it was written for a neurotypical person, giving me fifteen more minutes is not going to help me understand it.

I would like more representation, more neurodiverse teachers. Not just someone who I can identify with but who can help me learn because they understand.

I would like more understanding about what it's like to be me, to be so different and how that affects my daily mental health trying to fit into a system that wasn't built for me to succeed.

I believe schools are not built to make you a better person, they are there simply to get you the best grades you can in order to get a job. It seems to me that schools are there for the people who are going to contribute to capitalism. They are built to help the people who are going to contribute to society and 'succeed' and inhibit those who don't. They don't want people there who can't achieve. They teach you how to get you to the next place in life, but without teaching you how to cope when you are there. They might be able to get me into university, but how am I going to cope with the workload there if they haven't given me the skills to deal with the workload now? Giving me extra time in an exam doesn't help me in the long run. Teach me life skills, how to learn, how to revise, how to remember. They are all far more useful skills that could give me so many more opportunities in the future.

As I said before, schools are not designed for neurodiverse people. We cannot learn in an environment set up for 'normal people'. My mum talks about us being the square pegs trying to fit into round holes. But you can't just shave my edges off to fit in the hole or keep bashing until I get through. Things need to actually change. If the school system was flipped around and designed for us, the neurodiverse, the square pegs, then everyone else could still learn. Everyone else wouldn't be at a disadvantage from being taught and assessed in a way that suits us.

We could change, we can change, so why don't we?

30

YOU AND ME (A POEM)

Written by Anita Kate Garai
Illustrated by Ben Oag

In this chapter we will have a look at a poem about diversity and inclusion, followed with a mindful contemplation.

You and Me

Here's a little poem.

When you read it, you will see,

that all of us are simply

me and you and you and me.

Some of us are quiet,

some are brash

and some are loud.

Some of us feel full of shame

and some of us feel proud.

For some it's really hard at school,
for some it's an easier ride.
Some of us pretend we're fine
but hurt down deep inside.

Some of us have lots of friends,
but still can feel alone.
Some of us stay at the back.
We prefer to be unknown.

Some of us are sad
and some are happy as can be.
Some of us have challenges
you may not even see.

There are people in our school
who want to say a quick hello.
They may remind you of yourself,
or someone that you know.

Hi, I'm Lin
and I'll begin,
by telling you what I love.
It's those really fancy glitter pens,
they're a gift sent from above!

Hey, what's up?
My name is Krupp.
I rarely say a word.
I have very little confidence,
so I'm hardly ever heard.

I'm Rahul.

I don't like school.

I'm always getting in trouble.

I just can't keep to all the rules.

My head gets in a muddle.

I'm Ameer.

I love it here.

It's where my best mates are.

I'm seriously bored at home,

I prefer it here, by far.

Hi, I'm Cade

and I'm afraid

of noises I don't know.

They make me want to run and hide,

so kindly let me go.

Hey, I'm Schwartz

and I love sports.

I play football every day.

I can't wait for the bell to ring,

so I can go and play.

My name is Caize.

There are many days

I find it hard to breathe.

When I'm in pain, it hurts so much.

Be patient with me, please.

I'm Miss Bunch

and I serve lunch.

I take pride in what I do.

My favourite food is sausage and mash,

and I love a good veggie stew.

Yo! I'm Star,

I'm the best by far.

Everyone knows I'm smart.

But out at play, I sit alone

and it hurts deep in my heart.

My name's Kai.

I'm really shy,

so please don't make me talk.

Please don't make me stand there,

while all my classmates gawk.

Hey, I'm Rae

and I should say

that shouting makes me scared.

My skin goes numb and my head goes blank,

especially if I'm unprepared.

Hi, I'm Lou

to be honest with you,

I'm feeling really stressed.

My parents always tell me

that I have to be the best.

I'm Shahid,

and I'm the kid

that everyone calls 'the clown',

but it's hard to keep pretending

on the days I'm feeling down.

I'm Mrs Higgs,

I've got three kids

although you wouldn't know it.

The truth is that I'm always tired,

but I hardly ever show it.

Hey, I'm Dwight,

I work day and night

I'm sometimes called a swot,

but I want to be a doctor

– it's a crazy dream I've got.

I'm Solomon.

My family's from

a place that's torn by war.

We had to leave, to save our lives

and I miss my life before.

Hey, I'm Bard.

I find it hard

to spell and read and write,

but I love to make up stories

when I lay in bed at night.

My name's Yan.

I'm from Japan.

I got hurt when I was one.

My left leg's longer than my right,

so I wobble when I run.

Stefan's my name

and dancing's my game.

I love to get up and move.

I can't sit still for very long,

'cos I need to find my groove!

I'm the girl

with all the curls

that everyone wants to touch.

But please, I'm really begging you – ask first.

Thanks very much.

I'm Mr Chad

and I'm feeling sad,

I've just been through a divorce.

It's hard to come to work each day,

but I get on with it, of course.

Hey, I'm Rees

and I'm Shanice.

School's our favourite place.

Our life at home is really hard,

but at school we both feel safe.

You see ...
we're all just doing what we can
and finding our own way,
and we all need different things
to help us get through every day.

So let's be patient with each other
and as kind as we can be.
'Cos as I said, we're all just
me and you
and you and me.

by Anita Kate Garai

Here are some exercises and reflections on the poem 'You and Me'

- Do you recognise yourself in any parts of the poem? (Alternative: Do any parts of the poem remind you of yourself?) Remember they may not match exactly, but may have some similarities.

- Do you recognise someone you know? Remember they may not match exactly, but may have some similarities.

- Find a part of the poem that you are drawn to.

- Read it again slowly, and this time as you read, notice any responses in your body. You may feel tightness, tension somewhere, aches, pains, tingling, fogginess, heat, cold, nothing, relaxation, an emotion rising, your breathing may change – or something else.

- See if you can just sit with whatever you feel and simply allow it to be here. Gently say hello to whatever you are feeling. There is no right or wrong.

- Resist the temptation to find meaning in any of your body's responses or create stories around them. Just see if you can be with the feelings as they are.

- You can repeat this exercise with another part of the poem, or even with the whole poem.

- What is it like to do this? What happens inside you, when you let the feelings be here, without trying to fix them, ignore them or change them in any way?

INDEX